38.95

D0389961

GENDERED MEDIA

CRITICAL MEDIA STUDIES

Institutions, Politics, and Culture

Series Editor
Andrew Calabrese, University of Colorado

GENDERED MEDIA

Women, Men, and Identity Politics

Karen Ross

Rowman & Littlefield Publishers, Inc.
Lanham • Boulder • New York • Toronto • Plymouth, UK

Published by Rowman & Littlefield Publishers, Inc.
A wholly owned subsidiary of
The Rowman & Littlefield Publishing Group, Inc.
4501 Forbes Boulevard, Suite 200, Lanham, Maryland 20706
www.rowmanlittlefield.com

Estover Road, Plymouth PL6 7PY, United Kingdom

British Library Cataloguing in Publication Information Available

Library of Congress Cataloging-in-Publication Data
Ross, Karen, 1957–
   Gendered media : women, men, and identity politics / Karen Ross.
      p. cm. — (Critical media studies)
   Includes bibliographical references and index.
   ISBN 978-0-7425-5406-1 (cloth : alk. paper) — ISBN 978-1-4422-0104-0
(electronic)
   1. Mass media and sex. 2. Sex differences in mass media. 3. Sexism in
mass media. 4. Women in mass media. 5. Gender identity in mass media.
I. Title.
P96.S45R67 2010
305.3—dc22   2009036586

∞™ The paper used in this publication meets the minimum requirements of
American National Standard for Information Sciences—Permanence of Paper
for Printed Library Materials, ANSI/NISO Z39.48-1992.

Printed in the United States of America

CONTENTS

ACKNOWLEDGMENTS

When colleagues have asked what I've been working on recently, and I tell them, "a book on gender and media," some of them say, "what, another one?" I can't imagine anyone saying, what, *another* book on the Internet/war/politics/music? That there are slightly more than a handful of books on aspects of the relationship between gender and media, between women, men, and media, says something about the large gap in the literature, which is gradually being filled by these wonderful and vibrant blooms. So I would like to thank my publishers for having the foresight to commission the book and for sticking with it (and me) when I got distracted by other things. In particular, I would like to thank Brenda Hadenfeldt (who has since left for pastures new) and her replacement, Niels Aaboe. I also want to thank Andrew Calabrese, the series editor, who pitched the idea to me many moons ago when we shared some pleasant space in Brazil. Throughout the years I have enjoyed productive interactions with my students on many of the themes rehearsed in this book, most often in classes which appeared to have nothing to do, at least superficially, with gender; this book is the better for their insights. I have also had the great good fortune to work with some wonderful colleagues who have since become good friends, including Carolyn Byerly, Virginia Nightingale, Marjan de Bruin, and

Julia Hallam:. sharing food and thoughts with these women and the many other friends and colleagues along the way has helped shape my understanding of the tricky and complex relations between women, men, and media. Thank you all.

In addition, I would like to thank Carolyn Byerly, for permission to reprint some material from two chapters (chapters 3 and 5) from one of our coauthored books, *Women and Media: A Critical Introduction* (2006); and to the publishers of that book, Wiley-Blackwell.

INTRODUCTION

Women's representation in the media will not be improved by increasing the number of women journalists, or by getting rid of the
worst excesses of sexism in advertising. What it actually requires is
a wide-scale social and political transformation, in which women's
rights—and women's right to communicate—are truly understood,
respected and implemented both in society and at large by the media. (Gallagher 2001, 7–8)

Any book which has "gender" in its title is likely to talk about power,
patriarchy, and culture. Any book which has "media" in its title is likely
to talk about influence, hegemony, and institutions. Where a book has
both these concepts in the title, then the reader can expect that all the
above will be discussed within its pages and, in this particular book,
framed within a critical and interpretive approach which teases out the
complexities between these different concepts. So it is that I start with
this ambition for this text and hope that by focusing on those aspects
of the tricky relationship between gender and media which interest me
particularly, I can contribute a few modest insights to a body of literature which explores the gendered dimension of all things media.

I began the thinking about, if not the writing of, this book a few days
after then British prime minister Tony Blair made political history by

winning a third term for "new" Labour on May 5, 2005. As I flicked idly through the pages of the reasonably serious British Sunday newspaper, the *Observer*, three days after his victory to get the lowdown on how the elections had played out, I became increasingly conscious of a peculiar gender absence. As someone who has spent the past fifteen years researching aspects of gender and media, I should not have been surprised, but it was the scale of women's invisibility which I found disconcerting, given the number of high profile women who were contesting seats in the election. On the second page of the *Election Special* supplement (the cover page was given over to a clever photograph of an improbably solitary Blair striding toward the door of No. 10) was a double-page analysis of the Labour Party's trials and tribulations during the campaign. As I read the patchwork of prose, I realized that its various elements exemplified exactly why gender *still* matters, why studying the ways in which women and men are represented by the media is important, why interrogating news discourse in particular to expose both crude and subtle biases continues to dominate my own research priorities. The writer of the first part of the analysis was one of the *Observer*'s regular journalists, Euan Ferguson, who in his second paragraph uses the word *girl* to describe a woman journalist from the BBC and ends it with a description of Tony Blair "and his wife Cherie." Now, OK, this *is* an accurate description of Cherie's status qua Tony, but after eight years on the international political stage there can't be many people who need Ferguson to tell them that Cherie is Tony's better, cleverer, and more intelligent half, so why the possessive *"his"* wife? Elsewhere in the spread, twelve individuals provide a thumbnail sketch on how it (the elections) was for them, ranging from B list celebrities to academics to campaigners to student activists. Perhaps there is no need for equal numbers of women and men to be asked to ruminate on the meaning of life, but really, why are only two of the twelve commentators women? Do women have nothing to say? I admit I do have a slight tendency toward the conspiracy thesis but why, in the rest of Ferguson's piece, does *every* mention of defeated candidates refer only to vanquished women? The Labour Party lost forty-plus seats in that particular election and most of the losers were men.

What this small anecdote signals, to me at any rate, is why gender still matters as an analytical category, why media still matter as players in the communication process, why researching the gender-media dyad is still an important project for media scholars. If thoughts of Tony Blair and Euan Ferguson were part of the starting point of this book, then its final drafting took place against the background of the U.S. primaries and subsequent presidential election in late 2008. Once again, the media's fascination with the other—this time the interesting competitive othering between race and gender (Obama and Clinton) and gender and class (Clinton and Palin)—was played out in the pages and broadcasts of the national and international media. Gender, race, and class were individually and collectively invoked as journalists and politicians alike traded cheap shots and dirty washing: the circus which is now the modern election campaign was further energized by prurient speculations over Sarah Palin's progeny, Hillary Clinton's husband, and Obama's religious affiliations.

Thirty-plus years and a whole lifetime ago, Gaye Tuchman and her colleagues published one of the first studies of women's representation in popular media and they made a statement that had a powerful resonance with women's lived experiences at that time (Tuchman, Daniels, and Benét 1978). This was that women were subject to "symbolic annihilation" by the media because they were mostly absent from news discourse and when they *were* made visible, they were often rendered childlike and/or in need of men's protection, or else consigned to the home as their only legitimate domain. The media's representation of women *has* changed since then, the picture *is* different, but this book explores the extent to which that change signals genuine progress rather than the replacement of one set of stereotypes for another. It's certainly different now, but is it better?

For sure, the years 2000–2009 (or the noughties) have heralded fast and furious developments in media products, technologies, and institutions. Notions of gender have morphed and shifted as ambiguity, ambivalence, and innovations in surgical procedures fracture the fixity of woman/man, feminine/masculine, gay/straight, and the knowing *performance* of gender (following Butler 1990) challenges biological essentialism. The landscape of gendered media relations has changed irrevocably over the past few decades as a result of both technological and cultural transformations and the kinds of questions and issues which concern us today are not necessarily the same as those which

preoccupied researchers in the past. This is a good thing of course, because society cannot stand still, but our understanding of now can only
really be meaningful if it is informed by our understanding of then. We
can make sense of much of the media's vilification of Hillary Clinton
and Sarah Palin by considering not only the concentration of media
ownership in the hands of a very few (male) players who are closely
aligned to the conservative right, but also by recognizing that the sexist
harassment and taunts of "loud-mouthed woman" is remarkably similar to the label of "noisy viragos" leveled against the suffragettes more
than one hundred years ago (Rake 2006) by the media establishment.
Women's magazines' preoccupation with the ultimate age-defying
face cream and cellulite-busting body lotion is merely the contemporary manifestation of a historical (for which read, *men's*) insistence
on women's bodily perfection. Women and men's different Internet
behaviors—with women mostly preferring discursive and relationship-
focused activities and men preferring action-oriented games—mirror
the more traditional sex-based behaviors we see manifest elsewhere in
society.

This book, then, take us on a journey to explore some of the ways in
which the media engage with gender, and vice versa. One book obviously cannot do everything and I am sure I will not please everyone in
my choice of foci, but as gender inflects everything we experience as
human subjects whether we recognize it or not, and as the personal is *always* political, I hope that some of the chapters please some of you some
of the time. So, what *do* I aim to achieve here? First, as with some of
the other texts which look at the gender-media relationship, a significant
proportion of the book is given over to discussions about representation.
Even if we subscribe to the view that the media actually have rather
less power than we first thought because we are now so thoroughly
media savvy that we can see through their cynical ploys to manipulate
us, media workers are not entirely without effect and some of what they
produce is certainly capable of provoking entirely contradictory readings among the consuming public. While it is undoubtedly possible to
view *Sex and the City* or *Desperate Housewives* as post-feminist, post-
ironic, post-modern commentary on the sexually liberated woman who
knows what she wants and knows how to get it, such shows can also be
read as fixing women to their biology, again, reducing their power to a

simply sexual ability to attract a suitable mate. Even as Carrie narrates her own epilogue at the end of the show, wryly showing us the depth of her self-awareness, she does so in her Barbie pumps and falling-off-the-shoulder vintage silk camisole. Such contradictory readings signal the complex ways in which notions of femininity and masculinity are traded in contemporary media and make clear the constructed nature of these sex-based renditions and thus the reason why "gender" appears in this book's title rather than "sex." It is precisely the disclosure or even *revelation* of these constructions which is a principal concern of this book, both in terms of making clear *how* gender—and here I mean constructions of both women and men—manifests in different ways in different media forms, together with making a few suggestions about *why* we get what we get and how we might work to get something different.

Issues of gender representation have been a major preoccupation of feminist media scholars for the past few decades and it is not just wishful thinking to suggest that gains have been made as a result of that work, so that what we see, read, and hear in popular media has been influenced by women's efforts to change their representational image (Byerly and Ross 2006). Part of that change is signaled in the ways in which the media have extended or updated some of their traditional notions of what being a woman or man means, so another ambition of this book is to look at shifting notions of identity. As we will see in the following pages, as society moves on so do the media, albeit a bit more slowly, and women and men now act out in nonstereotypical roles in all genres: women report from war zones, men host daytime talk shows. On the other hand, less positive aspects of this apparent smoothing out of sex-based differences show up in the ways, for example, in which young women are now framed as the principal actors in a range of "undesirable" behaviors such as binge drinking, underage smoking, and street fighting—girl power gone grotesque. But in the media's war of the sexes, women's muscle flexing is at the expense of men's potency, so stories of rude aggressive women are matched by others identifying a crisis in masculinity. As Gill (2007) points out, analyses which identify these trends as being either symptomatic of a backlash against feminism or else a celebration of the mainstreaming of feminist thinking, are both more or less true. Screening for breast cancer is a legitimate news item for the health correspondent to pursue. But at the same time, those self-same breasts appear in daily newspapers and are used to advertise perfume, couture, and toilet cleaner. The broadsheet press will now report stories about powerful women leaders but at the same time the number of older women appearing in advertisements is miniscule. We *can* see progress, but for many of us, it is painfully slow.

So far, this discussion has been about how the media frame us, as gendered subjects, but the other side of that media-gender coin is how we use the media, how we act as agents and architects of our mediated world. The final aim of the book, then, is to explore some of the ways in which we take control of media, through our production activities and especially our involvement in new information and communication technologies including website development and content. While much has been made about the progressive potential of the Internet, rather less attention has been paid to the ways in which gender inflects new technologies; this book seeks to remedy that gap in a modest way. These three gender-based concerns—representation, identity, and agency—thread through the following chapters, each becoming more or less prominent at different points in the unfolding narrative.

The other thread which binds the whole together is that of feminism itself, or rather, a discursive and analytical approach to interrogating media texts which is feminist in orientation. In saying this, I acknowledge straightaway that there is no single feminist theory but rather many feminisms and thus feminist theories. The terms *feminism* and *feminist* have undergone considerable scrutiny, argument, and transformation in meaning over time, particularly in relation to the linking of those terms to a white Western bourgeois theoretical position and lived experience. Women of color have questioned precisely the Anglocentric privilege which the twin terms connote (see, for example, Hill-Collins 1990), identifying the double disadvantage (gender/race, sexism/racism) which women of color experience, even as the shared experience of *being women* is acknowledged. One response to the problem of feminism's color has been the construction of new terms such as *womanist*; in this case appropriating a term made popular by the African American writer Alice Walker in the 1980s, invented to signify a woman who is committed to the survival of her whole people, men and woman. Such new terms attempt to link feminist struggles to a broader political agenda which seeks to fight racism, economic exploitation, and other forms of oppression (see also Johnson-Odim 1991). A flavor of this debate is another theme which slides through the book's pages at various points. However, I should be clear and say that, although incredibly important, issues of race, ethnicity, and racism are not given equal weighting with gender, even though signposts are made to literatures which do indeed foreground these matters more explicitly.

I recognize that in the late 2000s, some commentators suggest we are now living through an age of "third-wave feminism," which appears to appropriate the postmodern turn in promoting an "anything goes as long as we're enjoying ourselves" ethos. I cannot accept the legitimacy of a position calling itself "feminist" when it is so consciously self-absorbed and politically bankrupt. So, in declaring what the book seeks to do, I should declare my own position, which is more in line with second-wave feminism—seeking equality for women and men through social trans-formation—where I simultaneously recognize the significant battles won but also the goals yet to be achieved.

The first chapter considers the shifts in our understanding of gendered identities, how the media frame women and men in contemporary dis-course and how we ourselves are challenging traditional renditions of what it is to be woman and man by performing gender to suit ourselves. The gains that feminists and others have secured over the past few de-cades, as well as women's increasing economic independence, have pro-voked a number of responses in the media, often paradoxical in nature. For example, new forms of gendered identity are now peddled, such as the sexy "new" femininity which sees women wearing conspicuous cleav-age and bling to the office, while at the same time concerns are expressed over men's ability to perform their "traditional" role in society. I there-fore consider some of the ways in which new forms of gendered identity are being constructed in and by the media, including notions such as the "new lad" and third-wave feminists and the rise of the men's lifestyle magazine. The chapter also considers how these media constructions are being challenged by individuals through alternative modes of self-expression, particularly as enacted through and enabled by new tech-nologies. The relative anonymity offered by the Internet, for example, allows the performance of different kinds of gendered identity, allows us to be whoever we want; we can disguise any and all our biological char-acteristics in favor of an avatar of our own form and choosing.

Chapter 2 returns us to more traditional turf and focuses on the various ways in which the media show interest in our corporeal selves, peddling narrow versions of acceptable femininity and masculinity and generally encouraging us to believe that a disciplined body is a good body. We are thus considerably less than the sum of our body parts. I explore the bodily discourses which circulate endlessly through popular text-based genres such as lifestyle magazines and advertisements, linking gendered identities to conventional prescriptions of acceptable bodily architecture. I also discuss the ways in which advertising as a specific set of representational practices is significantly involved in the perpetuation of particular and idealized renditions of femininity and, increasingly, masculinity (in both cases read, young, white, Western, beautiful), which function to make all but a very few of us see ourselves as constant works in progress, endlessly open to cosmetic, surgical, and other kinds of bodily improvement. The chapter then goes on to discuss the impact of these stylized renditions of self on ordinary women and men, looking specifically at discourses around obesity, size zero, and the six-pack as ways into understanding the preoccupation with bodily weight and the social prescription that less is more. Finally, we look at some of the ways in which these dangerous obsessions are being challenged, including by parts of the beauty industry itself, even as these challenges are open to ridicule and accusations of a sense-of-humor bypass and/or tragic misunderstandings of the new, noughties zeitgeist.

Thirty years on from second-wave feminism, the contemporary debates around sex in/and media, and especially in popular culture, are almost the same as those earlier ones, with both sides as entrenched as they ever were. Mapping these debates and their various proponents and detractors is the topic of chapter 3. On the one hand stands a discourse which says society has become little more than a Hefneresque "pornosphere" with sex oozing out of every media pore, where men beat up on women as they confuse the public presentation of the endlessly available airbrushed semi-naked model with the ordinary woman on the street or in her home. The commodification of the sexualized female body, used to sell anything from cars to perfume to jeans to toilet cleaners, is seen as contributing to an increase in sexual violence against women, as the persistent circulation of such images provokes both arousal and contempt. In the other corner are the "anything-goes" contingent, who celebrate this newfound sexual liberty as signaling the end of sexual repression and the smuttiness of the dirty postcard. For supporters of the so-called sexual revolution in the mediascape, the casual trade in sexually explicit material demonstrates a wholesome and natural way of enjoying looking and doing sex, on-screen, in magazines, in the press, online, everywhere. Viva fornication! This chapter therefore aims to map the debates about sex and/in the media which have taken place over the past few decades and to explore the politics of the pornographic which animate those debates, both consciously and implicitly. It also considers some of the contemporary manifestations of our fascination with the sexually explicit, including web-based sex sites and some of the materials and products which are aimed at a specifically female audience.

A focus on news media's coverage of women is the substance of chapter 4, especially the ways in which, despite the incursion of women into news industries including into senior positions, what we see, hear, and read continues to be news about men. As we approach the end of the first decade of the new millennium, I realize that I have been researching the relationship between gender and news for fifteen years and my analyses today are depressingly similar to the ones I made in the early 1990s. This is not to say that absolutely nothing has changed over the past few decades or so, because there *have* been some significant gains, mostly as a result of fearless campaigning by women both within and without the news industry, but change has been slow and piecemeal. Chapter 4 thus looks at this question in more depth, first by outlining some basic ideas about the constructed nature of news and the ways in which journalists, either wittingly or otherwise, persistently use a narrow range of "frames" which stereotype women. It then considers some of the historical research on women and news, showing the ways in which over time and across continents women are rendered almost invisible in mainstream news discourse and that when they do appear are seldom granted autonomy but instead are more usually framed as victims, trophy wives, or girlfriends. Specific analyses of three sets of relationships then follow, which focus on women/politics/media; women as sources in news articles; and women as newsworkers, including their experiences of workplace harassment.

Returning to thoughts of the Internet and its revolutionary potential as a communications medium, chapter 5 considers the relationships which women and men have with the Internet, how they behave online, as well as the exponential rise of websites which are targeted toward a female-consuming public. The ferociously evolving technology which is the Internet has been preoccupying media researchers since at least the 1990s, with commentators euphorically optimistic about the technology's potential or mordantly disturbed by its perversions, in almost equal measure. In this chapter, we focus on those aspects of the Internet which are specifically concerned with gender and gender difference, in particular, how women and men do different things when online, the gendered aspects of the digital divide, how women and men talk to each other and between themselves, how women network, and the development of women-friendly websites. How women and men (differently) experience the Internet is important for its future development, especially in terms of how we, as both consumers and increasingly producers of web-based content, might exert influence over its future direction. Historically, women have found it difficult to come to voice in media contexts, let alone exercise any power over shaping the contours of the media landscape, but does the general lack of gatekeeping across the virtual sky enhance our ability to nudge the medium in ways which were and are simply unthinkable in terms of traditional media? Ways, moreover, which begin to subvert the gendered power relations which characterize most every other aspect of our social, cultural, and economic lives, moving us toward a more inclusive environment where our voices, in all their glorious timbres, can be heard. Some of these issues are discussed in this chapter where I rehearse aspects of the current debates about the possibilities and practices of a gendered (cyber)space.

The concluding chapter draws the threads of all these various arguments together but also explores how women have challenged mainstream media's propensity toward stereotype and status quo. Importantly, although the media do exert considerable power in their repetitive circulation of particular versions of "acceptable" femininity and masculinity, they do not have it all their own way. The Internet in particular but also other technologies are being successfully appropriated by both individuals and groups to provide alternative visions of our sexed selves.

As a final point and before we get into the substantive discussions which follow, it is perhaps worth returning to where we began, with a short comment on my ambitions for this book, or rather, what it does *not*

attempt to do. Most books which focus on the relationship between gender and media are often focused exclusively on women, where "women/
femininity" becomes synonymous with "gender." While this book does
indeed discuss men as well as women and can thus use the word *gender*
in its title with a degree of confidence, it does not move very far into the
more ambiguous terrain of sexual identity beyond the familiar notions of
femininity and masculinity, such as queer and the trendier metrosexual.
While issues such as sexuality, ethnicity, race, disability, and age are
discussed within and across all the chapters to different degrees as they
work with and through gender, none of these identity traits have a chapter to themselves. I identify the book's orientation here not to reveal its
limitations so much as to signal that any text is a product of its author's
own interests and preoccupations: I hope you share some of mine.

> The more I read in the papers about how awful everyone thinks [my
> blonde hair] is, the more determined I feel to stick to it!
>
> —Lily Allen, on accepting *Glamour* magazine's
> Editor's Special Award in 2008

I

PROJECT GENDER

Identity/ies in Flux

We allow our ignorance to prevail upon us and make us think we can survive alone, alone in patches, alone in groups, alone in races, even alone in genders.

—Maya Angelou

Not so long ago, or so we fondly imagine, women were women and men were men and everything in the garden was rosy. We knew our place in the social structure—men on top, women below—and although some of us kicked against the established order and campaigned for equality, assumptions about men's dominance, as head of household, primary breadwinner, and decision maker in both private and public spheres, remained remarkably stable. But recently, the gains that feminists and others have secured over the past three decades, and shifts in social relations including women's increasing economic independence, have provoked a number of responses in the media, often paradoxical in nature. For example, new forms of gendered identity are now peddled, such as the sexy "new" femininity which sees women wearing conspicuous cleavage and bling to the office as well as the club, while at the same time concerns are being expressed over men's ability to perform their "traditional" roles in society. Women's new authority is seen as destabilizing men's sense of themselves, provoking a contemporary debate about a so-called crisis of masculinity. From this view, men are no longer certain about their place in the world, of how they should be men in an environment where not only are women capable of earning their own wage and running their own homes, but can also have children by artificial means, thus circumventing even the most basic of men's biological purposes. This "crisis" has manifested itself in different ways, from shifts in individual men's behavior, to group responses, to popular media reactions. Women have also been affected, with appeals to help men work through their angst, playing to traditional notions of women's inherent nurturing talents. As it is women's independence which has caused the crisis in the first place, they are seen as responsible for finding solutions, not least by sublimating their own desires in order to cherish those of men. While some women are saying FCUK to being told to get back in their box, others appear to be taking this attributed blame to heart. This opening chapter thus considers some of the ways in which new forms of gendered identity are being constructed in and by the media. It also explores how these media constructions are being challenged by individuals (women and men) through alternative modes of self-expression, particularly as enacted through new technology.

A NEW MORAL PANIC: MASCULINITY IN CRISIS

In a number of different ways, contemporary (factual) media representations of masculinity often frame men as dysfunctional and/or in crisis. As Segal (2006) points out, part of the problem of contemporary masculinity is that as long as the traditional "normative" cultural and social ideas of manhood privilege power, rationality, and assertiveness as the primary markers of man, then many men live in fear of being unmasked as unmanly. Importantly, though, the *real* differences in achievement and success in life are not between women and men but between men and other men, and key influences in determining that success or failure are demographic in nature, such as class, ethnicity, and age. Thus, while men's lifestyle magazines certainly encourage their male readers to look at women in hypermasculinized (sexist) ways, their use of male celebrities and features on financial and/or social success also encourage men to look at other men in ways guaranteed to force a comparison with self. If that self is found wanting because it is not, say, as successful, attractive, fit, rich, or conventionally masculine as those guys parading before them on the pages of the glossies, then this could feed into a destructive self-perception, resulting in overly macho behavior or a retreat into depression, both of which play well into the idea of masculinity in crisis. But what *is* this crisis, really, and how did it happen, or rather, why are men so often framed in this way? One of the primary "causes" for the crisis is named, unsurprisingly, as "woman," whose ambitious drive for a place at the decision-making table (culturally, socially, politically, and economically) is damaging men's sense of themselves. In her latest book, *What Makes Women Happy*, erstwhile feminist turned conservative matron Fay Weldon has some interesting advice for women,

> If you are happy and generous-minded, you will fake it [orgasm] and then leap out of bed and pour him champagne, telling him, "You are so clever" or however you express enthusiasm. . . . Faking is kind to male partners. . . . Otherwise they too may become anxious and so less able to perform. Do yourself and him a favor, sister: fake it. (cited in Hill 2006, n.p.)

Weldon's retrograde analysis puts women back into the corset from which they have only recently fought their way free, turning them back into whores in the bedroom and angels in the kitchen. The slut-saint dichotomy is perfectly captured by the advertising industry's shorthand for advertisements which feature women demonstrating kitchen products—TTK—or, Two Tarts in a Kitchen; Nigella Lawson in a see-through blouse. Weldon's analysis also requires woman (especially in her role as partner) to take on another role—therapist—for the problem child her man has now become. Similarly, in Lyons and Willott's (1999) study of men's health discourse in one British newspaper, they found that men were mostly associated with work and culture and women were associated with nature and health. In other words, women were more "naturally" inclined toward health giving and nurturing and were therefore made responsible (by the newspaper at least) for keeping men healthy. Importantly, it was assumed that men were embarrassed to admit that they worried about their own health or did anything proactive to look after themselves; a strategy which once again calls on women to perform this function for them. In most advertisements for medicines or health products, women figure almost exclusively as the givers of remedies to family members, playing into normative stereotypes of woman as earth mother and nurturer and bracketing men with children as recipients of "mother's care."

If men are no longer the primary breadwinner, no longer undisputed head of the family, no longer sole initiator of sexual contact, no longer even necessary for the act of procreation, then what *is* their role in the world? Popular media plays around with the idea of masculinity in crisis in many different forms, from articles in both women's and men's magazines, the reporting of therapeutic men's groups and the presentation of the useless man stereotype in so-called post-ironic ads. In some car ads, for example, the man is shown to be interested in color and fabric whereas the woman is interested in torque and spark plugs. There are contradictions here between the mythic trope of man-as-warrior and those of man-in-crisis or even the non-macho-man, which the media circulate unproblematically and without comment. Perhaps this signals the media's more sophisticated understanding of the paradox of contemporary life or, more likely, a lack of interest in the implications of trying to work it all through.

BOYS BEHAVING BADLY: THE NEW LAD AS POOR BABY IN MEN'S MAGS

One very popular version of modern masculinity, at least in the United Kingdom, is that of the "new lad." This, and its practice, "laddism," is usually associated with the development of a particular genre of men's magazine, specifically, "lads' mags," exemplified by titles such as *FHM* (For Him Magazine) and *Loaded* and their later imitators, *Nuts* and *Zoo*. While these titles are British, they have a print circulation considerably beyond the shores of the United Kingdom and their web versions are obviously accessible to a global male audience. Importantly, their content has a universal appeal, focusing on "typical" male preoccupations with sex, smut, and soccer. The idea of the lad as less than an adult man is perfectly captured in the way in which these magazines celebrate the juvenile masculinity of their imagined audience, where the reader is in a state of "extended adolescence, in which irresponsibility, hedonism and heterosexual lubricity are a condition of entry" (Tincknell et al. 2003, 50). In the same way that women's magazines have always constructed particular renditions of femininity they want their readers to emulate— usually requiring the purchase of something which will, finally, give them the dream body/lifestyle/partner, they crave—so men's magazines also peddle a fantasy. Here, though, men's concerns (now constructed through the logic of the "crisis in masculinity") are addressed, mostly implicitly, by the provision of various coping strategies where men can perhaps retrieve a vestige of their former power and thus their sense of what it means to be a man in the twenty-first century.

So, what advice do men receive within the pages of those magazines targeted specifically at them? How is masculinity explained and demonstrated? Well, to some extent, as with women's magazines, different magazine genres produce differently nuanced narratives, so that lads' mags such as Loaded,[1] Nuts, and Zoo have a different look and feel to, say, FHM[2] or GQ (Gentleman's Quarterly). However, the sense of masculinity is often very similar, even if the language and images might vary—leaving aside the more factual articles about archetypically men's stuff such as sport, cars, and drinking—the other major discursive preoccupation to be found is focused on men's relationship with women. Our sexual selves are nearly always understood in relation to each other (Connell 1995), so in men's magazines, masculinity is discussed in relation to femininity, hence the preponderance of content devoted to the abidingly complicated notion of intimate (for which read almost exclusively heterosexual) relationships.

If we agree with Butler (1990), then gender is something we *perform* rather than something that we *have* or something we *are*. In other words, gender is entirely constructed and we "do" gender through the playing out of any number of "scripts" which we have both consciously and unconsciously internalized. Thus, exploring how men's magazines encourage men to do masculinity in particular ways should provide some insights to why intimate relations seem so fraught and fragile. Popular media persistently circulate models of sexual identity, offering up an endlessly varied (if determinedly heterosexual) menu from which we can choose, and men's magazines are no exception. However, as a genre, they are a relatively new phenomenon; the existence of which suggests a new uncertainty about men's place and meaning in contemporary life. For example, more than twenty years ago Ferguson (1983) argued that the genre's absence from the magazine scene indicated that men needed no directions about how to perform their gender identity before the early 1990s. But in a contemporary environment which is far less fixed, the ambiguities around men's role appear partially resolved by the form of address to "everyman" which men's magazines articulate, offering off-the-shelf solutions to men's relationship problems, what Jackson, Stevenson, and Brooks (2001) describe as a conceptual map, which helps men navigate the tricky landscape of personal relationships and the performance of masculinity.

In her study of *Loaded* and *FHM* magazines, Rogers (2005) suggests that one of the key ways in which relationships are "handled" and discussed is through the use of working practices, legalistic and scientific metaphors, so that men are shown how to master intimacy as just another everyday task to perform. Much of the advice is humorous, for example, the Meeting of New Women Act and the Long Term Relationship Accord, where the various principles enshrined in these faux laws prescribe how men should behave toward women. But these are juxtaposed by other kinds of advice which make clear that the real goal of mastering intimacy is more about sexual conquest than the development of a relationship, for example, "Get her a little bit pissed, . . . she'll respond quicker" (*Loaded* 2002, June, 58); or "Get even the most unreceptive of women ready and willing in 60 seconds!" (*FHM* 2002, May, 136). While Rogers did find evidence of less crude approaches to relationships, an important aspect of relationship discourse was the attempt to bring control over chaos, knowledge over ignorance, so that men achieve a better understanding of how to "do" relationships which satisfy women but which do not require men to sacrifice that part of themselves associated with a sense of powerful masculinity. "This discourse secures the reader's position on the properly masculine side of the emotion/action dichotomy. Relationships are taken out of the private realm, extinguishing its feminine connotations, and placed, alongside employment and the law . . . , securely in the domain of public life" (Rogers 2005, 193). What is interesting in Rogers's analysis is her identification of the "rules of engagement" as part of relationship etiquette because not only do such ideas connote a kind of playfulness in advice-giving but they also protect magazines from accusations of sexism by appealing to a post-ironic sensibility. This kind of distancing strategy, which avoids taking relationships too seriously, is frequently employed in men's magazines more generally, not just the ones which are self-consciously lads' mags. For example, *Men's Health*, a highly popular magazine in Europe, features a section titled "Man to Man" where men can get relationship advice from a virtual "mate" rather than having to spend time with real friends, either women or men, and therefore having to expose their anxieties (Boni 2002).

What then do these magazines tell us about "doing" masculinity in the contemporary world? What both lads' mags and their less overtly sex-saturated stablemates demonstrate is a continuing ambiguity over what men are and what men do. On the one hand, men are given nudge-nudge-wink-wink permission to be the worst example of their Neanderthal past, grunting, farting, and play fighting in the forest with their mates before going back to the cave at night to have rough sex with the women who have waited patiently and open-legged for their return. On the other, copious advice is offered to resolve the crisis of masculinity, which plays out as stress and impotence—hey guys, this is not your fault, it's the mad world we live in—at the same time as grooming products, sharp tailoring, and the latest technological must-haves are peddled as exogenous ways to achieve satisfying manliness. If such products are promoted by celebrity footballer-types like Thierry Henri or David Beckham, then they are doubly blessed and desirable because permission to care about stubble rash comes via ruggedly masculine endorsement. Thus, the ambiguities and contradictions which exemplify current debates about what it means to be a man are manifest through the so-called post-ironic discourse of men's lifestyle magazines. While this comedic gaze attempts to disavow serious critique by purporting a tongue-in-cheek knowingness, it is clear that forms of mediated (mostly hegemonic) masculinity are constantly traversing different genres and formats, so the laddish male presenters of *Top Gear*[3] have copies of *Loaded* on the couch and *FHM* features full-page spreads of buffed-up celebrity pecs and abs. Fortunately, the cave dwellers don't have it all their own way, and the contradictions of hegemonic masculinity have been usefully examined and discussed in response to both the "crisis" in masculinity and the Neanderthal hoorah of shows like *American Chopper* (Beasley 2008; Carroll 2008; Gill 2009a;

Thompson 2008). The phenomenon of the "new lad" obviously predated the launch of *Loaded* and the magazine's antecedents can be seen, arguably, in some of the more overtly salacious British tabloids such as the *Sunday Sport*, which is soft-core porn masquerading as a newspaper—the *National Enquirer* meets *Playboy*. Both give men permission to retreat into their earlier, testosterone-filled adolescent selves, by their gleeful and considerable display of naked female flesh (the "nipple count") and the normalization of such displays. All good clean fun, boys will be boys, but the question which should concern us is how will they ever become men?

When the British tabloid the *Sun* began publishing photographs of topless women on page 3 in 1970, it paved the way for the routinization of displaying women's naked bodies in mainstream media not just in the United Kingdom but around the world. The newspaper's decision to set this particular trend was prompted, arguably, by a need to revive flagging sales, but that it thumbed its nose at the earnest politicking of second-wave feminism and a nascent political correctness were also plus-points for its supporters. Critics of page 3 were denounced as man-hating, old-fashioned, frumpy, boring, lacking a sense of humor/sense of the ironic, feminist/cultural dinosaur, and so on. These name-calling tactics function to disavow and undermine criticism, naming the feminist (and any other) challenge to casual porn as boringly last century, symptomatic of a humorless sensibility which just doesn't understand that bare breasts signify women's empowerment. Even Tony Blair wears "naked lady" cufflinks to show how cool he is, and sporting a copy of *Nuts* or even *Playboy* in a back pocket is almost de rigueur for the man-about-town: suddenly, porn is the hip new accessory for urban man.

Paradoxically, when launching *Nuts* in 2004, Mike Soutar, IPC's editorial director (publisher of *Nuts*), said that his market research showed that men were "blocked" from buying men's magazines because of the volume of unsubtle female nudity and bad language. Soutar insisted that *Nuts* would contain "simple" content, with extensive coverage of current affairs: "There's a boundary at which that becomes something which is a very solo pleasure rather than something that is socially acceptable to read on a bus or a train or leave lying around the house if you have kids" (Soutar quoted in Burrell 2004, 8). However, despite what Soutar said at the time of the launch, at the time of writing three years later, *Nuts* is

indistinguishable from other lads' mags, showing the same acres of naked female flesh, buffed-up body parts posed in stereotypical positions,
borrowing image styles from the repertoire of traditional pornography.
Some of us would argue that packaging soft-core sexual imagery as the
new cool, porno-chic meets post-irony in the post-feminist era, is clever
if cynical marketing. Promoting lads' mags in this way means that no
shame attaches to the reader because it's all good, clean, harmless fun,
and moreover, handling these goods, in every sense, actually signifies an
authentic and assertive masculinity.

Appropriating the discourse of irony, or even the post-ironic, in the
context of soft-focus porn is again a clever ploy but whether that is really what's going on is rather more questionable (Gill 2007). On the one
hand, the sheer macho posturing and sexism cannot possibly be taken
seriously, so is therefore applauded as a mere breathing space where the
display of sexuality can be viewed as playful (McNair 2002; McRobbie
2004). For Gauntlett (2002), irony in lads' mags is used to make men
feel OK about the reduced potency of masculinity in contemporary
society, hyping up the Neanderthal as a face-saving strategy to preserve
the (nevertheless still acknowledged) *illusion* of male superiority. Clever
stuff. On the other hand, claims of, "it's just irony, stupid," is seen
merely as a cynical strategy to derail and forestall criticism, allowing
magazines to peddle a discourse of self-mockery which is entirely dis-
ingenuous, allowing the expression of politically incorrect sentiment to
coexist with the simultaneous claim that this is not at all what is meant.
Here is irony as double-bluff, sexist backlash masquerading as knowing
parody where the symbols of male-ordered hyperfemininity are sold
back to us as a post-ironic, post-feminist playfulness which smugly dares
critics to find their voice and object. Magazine competitions which re-
ward the lucky winner with a "boob job" for his girlfriend must be read
as the playful appropriation of ridiculous male stereotypes even as, at
the same time, they illustrate the casual understanding of women as less
than the sum of their body parts. The trick is continued with the bluff-
double-bluff so that no matter how mockingly, men are ultimately seen
as amusingly (and really) irredeemable and thus given permission to
actually *be* as sexist or unreconstructed as they want and, as important,
as they actually *are*. This is evidenced perfectly in Stevenson, Jackson,
and Brooks's work with consumers of these magazines (2000, 383): "You

know, whether I want to start screwing around or whatever . . . it's okay to be this, this is actually who I am" (professionals, Islington) and, "it's sort of allowing you to say and think and talk about things you may have thought" (politics lecturer, Manchester).

But, leaving aside the problematic issue of what constitutes pornography, there are important issues of denotation and access because of what men's magazines say about the place of women in culture and society more generally. What men (or women for that matter) choose to read or do in the privacy of their own home is quite different to what I (or anyone else) might unintentionally access in my local supermarket or bookstore. The migration of soft-core porn magazines like *Nuts* or *Zoo* or *Fiesta,* from the top to the bottom shelf makes them accessible to anyone, children and adults alike. That *Fiesta* now jostles for space with *PC User*, *Cosmopolitan*, and *My First Pony* regularizes the consumption of women's bodies as just another hobby, the ultimate fast-food snack.

BACK-TO-BASICS OF A DIFFERENT KIND: MEN AND CAMPFIRES

The wider men's movement is a little short on irony and the binge-drinking, *Fightclub*-loving lout culture of the new lad is balanced in the media's mind by the overweening limp-wristedness of the diaper-changing, panini-eating, vacuum-wielding new man who used to be parodied in any number of U.K. and U.S. sitcoms and comedy series. But we don't really hear much about that soppy liberal kind of new man any more, as he has been replaced by more rugged and "authentic" versions of man-as-he-is-now. While the lad exemplifies one attempt to shore up a failing masculinity, another is a more grown-up and powerfully manly figure in the shape of the new "real" man, such as that offered by the Promise Keepers (PK), a quasi-religious men's movement which has an explicitly Christian mission to maintain traditional (for which read patriarchal) values, and to rejuvenate "godly manhood" (Bartkowski 2001, 33). The movement has received sustained criticism from several quarters, some detractors seeing it at the center of the antifeminist backlash and committed to reversing the gains which women have made over the past forty years and restoring patriarchy in the home (Jackson

1997; Messner 1997). Conversely, other commentators see nothing much wrong with PK's valorization of man-as-godhead, believing that its existence is symptomatic of contemporary man's malaise where his role in society is being compromised by women's advancement: "PK is overwhelmingly made up of ordinary men trying to figure out their place in a changing society, where work roles, family relations and personal identity are all in flux" (R. H. Williams 2001, 9). But if this is so, where are the women's movements clamoring for a return to domestic drudgery as the antidote for too much damn liberation?

Bloch (2001) is also willing to give PK the benefit of the doubt, arguing that although the seven promises which the PK brethren pledge are wreathed about by God and the Bible, women's involvement in ministry has had the positive impact of encouraging men's articulation of their feelings and willingness to discuss their emotions. Moreover, if holding to PK values makes men better husbands and fathers, PK could in fact have a positive impact on American society rather than a negative one. Well, yes, maybe, but Bloch's use of the term "better" raises rather more questions than the positive analysis can answer.

While the PK movement is currently too disparate, too internally and ideologically conflicted to pose a real threat to women's continued liberation from the yoke of patriarchy, America's fundamentalist, conservative, and evangelical heart beats ever more strongly, easily trouncing the wishy-washy liberals who call for an end to war, who support gay marriage and same-sex adoptive parents. The robust masculinity of the Promise Keepers, religious fundament notwithstanding, is evidenced most clearly in the places where they hold their rallies, that is, in sports stadia: muscular masculinity in the shape of sports stars adorns PK literature. However, Bartkowski (2001) suggests, paradoxically, that those most male of spaces take on an avowedly "feminine" complexion when PK rally members are encouraged to hug each other, weep together, and sing. But of course, these behaviors simply reflect the same rituals which men practice at real sports matches, aided and abetted by the athletes themselves who publicly emote, kiss, embrace, and take their clothes off as an integral part of the contemporary sports spectacle. Part of the success of the Promise Keepers has been to develop strategies to unite very different men from very different backgrounds, playing on notions of the good father and the good American, which transcend the otherwise troublesome points of conflict such as race, ethnicity, and socioeconomic background. Using popular cultural artifacts such as slickly produced magazines—*New Man: For Men of Integrity*—concert-style rallies, and religious bands makes the movement appear less zealous, less weird, and thus more attractive to "regular" guys (Lockhart 2001). While movements like the Promise Keepers are undoubtedly complex and complicated, the media's response to them is not. For most news media, the Promise Keepers is a quasi-religion, whose members join because they are fed up with successful women and want to practice in the home what they can no longer do in their work environment, that is, exercise dominion over people, in this case their families.

But the gains of feminism are only a small part of the story of men's new search for identity, and in fact a much wider social change over the past fifty years—significantly, the move from sole to joint income family units—has had more significant impact on men's social roles than the modest wins of feminism. Ironically, the slow lessening of the gender pay gap is due much more to men's decreasing average wage than women's increasing one, a situation that can only be seen as lose-lose.

Another "real-man" and North American–focused response to the crisis of masculinity and which again "blames" women are weekend warriors like the Mythopoetics, disciples of John Bly and other advocates of men's return to the woods (see Livingston 2007; Magnuson 2008). Unlike the Promise Keepers who have an explicitly Christian mission, the Mythopoetic movement is more spiritual in a New Age rather than religious sense of the word and is based on the belief that the modern man has been "psychically and spiritually wounded" (Williams 2001). Based on the writings of John Rowan (1987) and Robert Bly (1990), the guiding principle for the movement is that men need to find the wild man within, a visceral "he" which has been obscured by years of indulgent childrearing by mothers. But, fortunately, all is not lost and men can once again become the men they always could (and should) be by participating in male-only group therapy sessions in natural settings, like woods, which might involve story sharing, music making, and encounter-style therapy sessions. Performing such rituals can, argue Bly and Rowan, restore man's innate masculinity and allow him to embrace a positive male identity. The media have tended to mostly ignore the weekend warriors who indulge in this pursuit of the real man within, largely because they do not court publicity. However, the general trend toward conservatism which is exemplified by the Mythopoetics and their comrades is a worrying cultural trend as it speaks the language of reactionary discourse which reframe women and men as essentialized biological categories, blames women (again) for men's diminished confidence and lost status, and seeks to reestablish men's rightful superordinate position. Importantly, in this view, men are the real victims of social and cultural oppression and thus need sympathy and support (Ferber 2000).

While both these movements have a more or less exclusively white membership, the African American community has also been rather exercised by the loss of standards and discipline in society, and although not really a movement, the Million Man March was an important event in highlighting concerns and responses. On October 16, 1995, the Million Man March took place in Washington DC, receiving considerable media attention and provoking debate not just about the broader men's movement but the specifics of African American manhood. A key criticism of some of the other initiatives such as the Promise Keepers and the mythopoetic politics of John Bly has been precisely their ethnocentrism, no matter how unwitting the whiteness of their members may be. Here, with the Million Man March (MMM), was a consciously African American initiative which spoke to a uniquely ethnically marked experience, organized and headed up by the controversial figure of Minister Louis Farrakhan, (then) self-styled Leader of the Nation of Islam. While there was support, both by the public and the media, for the ethos of the MMM—a celebration of black economic independence and pride, self-discipline, and the importance of family (Pauley 1998)—there was considerable antipathy for its progenitor because of the controversy which surrounds Farrakhan.[4]

One of the more high profile supporters of the march who nevertheless stayed away because of Farrakhan's involvement was Colin Powell, more recently known for his involvement in George W. Bush's administration during the U.S. invasion of Iraq. Powell was concerned that his presence would lend credibility to Farrakhan, while at the same time he wanted to show solidarity with the marchers: "While I deplore the message of Minister Farrakhan, I cannot ignore what's happening in the presence of several hundred thousand African Americans who care about themselves, care about their future, care about the future of this country" (Powell quoted in the *New York Times*, October 17, 1995, A20). Interestingly, although the march did receive media coverage, for example, the *New York Times* ran twenty-one articles on the topic October 8–15, nearly all of them focused on the messenger-message problematic, rather than focusing on the purpose of the march itself (Watkins 2001). This again demonstrates the difficulty of campaign groups and/or organized protests attracting media interest for their goals (ends) rather than their methods of achievement (means). In this case, the aims of the march to focus attention on both the positive pride of the African American community as well as identify issues of discrimination were mostly ignored in favor of debating the competing views of the supporters and detractors of Louis Farrakhan and his political and race-inflected viewpoints. However, Henry (1998) argues that a significant indicator of the march's success was the testimonies of marchers who spoke of the personal (and positive) impact that their involvement in the march had on their lives subsequently, including developing a better relationship with their families. It is interesting to note that even with the focus on family the very obvious anomaly in the march's membership and indeed Farrakhan's call for action—the absence of women—remained unquestioned by the media.

The last men's group we are going to consider provides a corrective to both the new lad and the new patriarch, and these are the "dutiful dads," estranged from their children by divorce and now campaigning for a more equitable deal from the criminal justice system. Here is a compassionate version of contemporary man, one who is in touch with his feelings and, more important, takes his paternal responsibilities seriously, albeit that he is no longer involved in the day-to-day care of his children. Of course, the media only becomes interested in dutiful dad when he does something spectacularly newsworthy, such as throwing flour bombs at the British brime minster. In 2003, Matt O'Connor established the U.K. organization Fathers For Justice (F4J) in order to give structure and weight to his personal campaign for father's rights, initiated because he believed that mothers (and his wife in particular) were always the winners in custody battles. However, with a slogan taken directly from the title of a song by the Manic Street Preachers, "If you tolerate this, then your children will be next," the group made clear that they were ready for battle, and their campaign strategy became more extreme as they tried to get the media interested in their cause. This extremism culminated in throwing condoms packed with purple flour at the prime minister in May 2004 when members of the group gathered in the Strangers' Gallery in the British Parliament and lobbed their bombs over the edge of the parapet and on to the parliamentarians below. "We just want to get our message across. We've been struggling with various bodies for nine months, trying to negotiate things, but as they are not taking it seriously again we felt we had to return to this" (Guy Harrison, member of F4J, quoted in Seamark and Newling 2005. 9).

While the group can claim some success as a result of the media's interest in their antics (for example, the naming of the phenomenon of McDonalds' Dads, where fathers take their children to the restaurant during their contact visits and try to connect with their family), the media have been just as interested in the internal squabbles between some of the more extreme members (Womack 2006). Their cause has also been somewhat undermined by a public distaste for the more sensational aspects of their campaign: for example, the group was accused of plotting to kidnap Leo Blair, son of Tony, in early 2006. Members of F4J are also prone to dress up, often as heroic cartoon characters such as Batman, Robin, and Spiderman (the superhero campaign), and conduct rooftop protests, including at the Royal Courts of Justice in 2003 and Buckingham Palace in 2005. Arguably, members see themselves as heroes trying to right a terrible wrong (against them and their children), but the organization's founder recognizes that the group's taste for extreme stunts has begun to compromise public support. "We now have 12,000 members nationally and another 4,000 globally. . . . We have become a victim of our own success and we are now in danger of imploding. When I started it I didn't realize what I was creating" (O'Connor cited in Weathers 2005, 20). At the time of writing, the group still exists and is still campaigning. As with other such groups, F4J recognize the double-edged sword of publicity, that their cause will only continue to receive media (and therefore public) attention if they continue with their extreme actions. On the other hand, it is precisely the extremism which provokes hostility among the public, even if there is general sympathy for their position in relation to unequal access to children after divorce. In 2009, their website bears the legend, "A father is for life, not just conception," which is an obvious play on the animal charity's exhortation that, "A dog is for life, not just for Christmas," but the group's detractors could make much of the analogy.

AND NOW FOR SOMETHING COMPLETELY DIFFERENT—A GIRL'S OWN (MEDIATED) STORY

The media's opprobrium for the assertive campaigning for gender equality which characterized the 1960s and 1970s (known as second-wave feminism) has given way to the contemporary celebration of a new, dynamic, can-do womanhood (Hinds and Stacey 2001). This new brand of femininity is confident, sexy, sassy, and most definitely not victim. What is taken for granted in this vocabulary of the "new" is an environment which is post-feminist and post-ironic, slyly insinuating that gender equality has now been won so women can stop hating men and return to wearing the short skirts and lipstick which they have always, secretly, craved. Women's apparent power and authority is manifest through a self-conscious celebration of their innate femininity, most obviously demonstrated through a concentration on those bodily attributes which are self-evidently *not* male. Sometimes the media tout this shift as being not about a new femininity but as a new kind of feminism, specifically, third-wave feminism (Shugart, Waggoner, and Hallstein 2001).

The media have been assisted in their efforts to undermine what we might call "traditional" feminism, conceptualized as an avowedly political project, by the self-proclamation of allegedly third-wave feminist voices. For example, two collections of essays published in 1995 rejected what contributors believe were the pious ramblings of sulky white women who persistently cast men and patriarchy in the role of oppressor and themselves as eternal victim (Walker 1995; Findlen 1995). Instead, these young(er) third wavers celebrate differences of all kinds and speak of the importance of fluid identities including gender, sexual, and racial ambiguities. Importantly, a clear focus is on the individual rather than the collective, on feeling good about oneself rather than bad about a whole group, about chasing desire rather than denying attraction. While it is arguable that these sentiments, although quite legitimate in themselves, can be incorporated within an avowedly *political* movement such as feminism, which strives for (collective) social change, the hedonistic turn which it promotes has been taken to heart by many young women keen to distance themselves from their hairy harpy foremothers. More cynically, feel-good femininity/feminism has been appropriated by popular media to construct a new gender identity for women and to suggest that feminism has finally made it into the mainstream. But this is to buy into a lie, or at least a myth, that conflates femininity with feminism and that either or both, when annexed to sexual confidence, becomes synonymous with empowerment.

However, it should be noted that media support for new women is usually restricted to championing their right to bare their breasts (but not to breastfeed), going to work (but not once they have a child), and being a celebrity (but only if they keep themselves in shape). Girl power is just that, for girls. Grown-up women with careers, kids, and cellulite are, conversely, often the focus of sustained hostility by conservative newspapers. The press now insist on reporting stories of in-your-face-girl-power, of successful young women who are clever, articulate, and proud of their curves. Phil Hilton, editor of men's magazine *Nuts*, suggests that young women are lining up at his door to be photographed without their clothes on for the magazine, and that those who criticize *Nuts* for exploiting women are simply out of touch with young women's sexual liberalism (cited in Orr 2005).

In a trenchant and well-argued analysis of raunch culture, Levy (2005) suggests that although many women profess an interest in strip clubs, pornography, and drinking men under the table, such behavior is less about being one of the girls than about being part of the boys' club. In other words, the best way to show how damned empowered they are is for women to emulate the guys. Wearing "Fit Chick Unbelievable Knockers" (FCUK) across their breasts or toting a playboy bunny on their key ring and reading *Hustler* with their girlfriends are, in this version of girl power, symbols of women's empowerment which show a playful, post-ironic, knowingness which marks them out as cool, hip women who really are lovin' it! "There's a way in which a certain lewdness, a certain crass, casual manner that has at its core a me-Tarzan-you-Jane mentality can make people feel equal. It makes us feel that way because we are all Tarzan now, or at least we are all pretending to be" (Levy 2005, 93).

But can women's appropriation of all the boring old male-ordered stereotypes of "appropriate" femininity actually be empowering? Can women's objectification of their own bodies and those of other women be seen as progress because *we* are doing it to *ourselves* instead of being *done to* by men? If the means are different, then the ends are depressingly the same. The problem here with popular culture's rendition of the sexually liberated contemporary woman is her one dimensionality. It is not just cool to show cleavage at work or spend time learning how to shimmy up the pole, but is almost de rigueur if women want to avoid being relegated to the trash bin of failed and frumpy womanhood. Dressing like a porn star has somehow become a proxy for women's liberation (Levy 2005); one has morphed into the other in a strange twist of history which crashes power with pornography to produce the emancipated woman-about-town whose best friends are her Wonderbra, her dildo, and the cast of *Sex and the City*. When Amy Winehouse accepted her award for best British solo artist at the 2007 Brit Awards she was described as looking like a "hooker going through a style crisis" (anon. journalist quoted in Sauma 2007). This is celebrity, Jim, but not as we know it.

Without doubt, and without judgment, some women *do* like porn and cruising lap-dancing clubs but what about everyone else? Why should women imitate the most stereotypical male fantasies of femininity in order to wear the badge of Ms. Kool? Why should women be content with popular culture's definition of power—the power to be a sexual magnet to men—when they are denied the *real* power of decision making in the Senate, in the Fortune 500 (ten women CEOs in 2006), in the judiciary? What's wrong with this picture of female potency? What is being embodied is not so much a new kind of authentic and sexually liberated woman but a tilt at an approximation of a male-ordered sexy femininity which is about a look but not a feel, about style over substance, about consumption not redemption. While Gill (2009a) is absolutely right to question the eliding tendencies of critics who bemoan the sexualization of popular culture on the grounds that a more nuanced understanding is necessary, she still concludes that contemporary cultural practices are classist, racist, sexist, and homophobic. As Goldman (1992) argues rather persuasively, the media's (or perhaps advertisers') clever trick has been to rebrand femininity as feminism and to conflate consumption with personal agency—I shop therefore I am.

THE CHALLENGE WITHIN

Sometimes, though, the sexy and the political do inhabit the same female body. Many celebrity women, especially pop divas, have long been seen as (often unsuitable) role models to which women aspire, hence the fascination with and cultivation of porn-star chic, *pace* Christina Aguilera, Britney, and any number of identikit girl bands who wiggle and grind to the beat of their bass. However, some artists offer women a glimpse of another way of being successful, although excess in some form or other is never far away. Courtney Love and Madonna sport their tattoos, confess their addictions, and then write songs about their experiences. Lily Allen's girl-next-door persona sings the frustrations of the everyday, of an ordinary life, of ups and downs, of sex, drugs, and dangerous liaisons.

The point about these women is that they don't write and sing as victims but as survivors, as women who have something to say and, as important, an audience who wants to hear. They offer a way of understanding women's experiences in all their complexity, their stupidity, their wonderfulness, singing about personal relationships which are real and painful but, in the end, where resolution is on women's terms. These are important messages for women to hear, that they have agency, power, and autonomy not because they have wealth (because most of us do not) but because they have insight, which is within all of us. Interestingly, not only do women such as Courtney and Lily (as with their nonconformist foremothers such as Patti Smith and Janis Joplin) eschew traditional modes of subordinate femininity in their songs but also enact their politics in their real lives. When the prestigious music magazine *New Musical Express* positioned Beth Ditto at the number one spot in its annual "Cool List" in 2006, Lily Allen (who also featured) was outraged by the *NME*'s self-congratulatory crowing. In response to the magazine's editorial, that the Cool List winners were "living proof that you can still rock a crowd when you're wearing stilettos," Allen subsequently wrote in her blog: "I mean, how fucking patronising . . . is that all we are, stiletto wearing people? . . . and . . . you put Muse on the cover 'cause you thought that your readers might not buy a magazine with an overweight lesbian [a reference to Beth Ditto who fronts The Gossip] and a not particularly attractive looking me on the front" (cited in Sauma 2007, 4).

Such sentiments, expressed by women who are in the public eye, demonstrate the potency of the celebrity voice to be raised in influential protest, here revealing the taken-for-grantedness of men's positioning at the top of *any* list of importance, which frames women's inclusion therein as always unusual and thus noteworthy. As such, these views provide useful correctives to the more frequent rehearsal of normative, sexy, femininity which sees women (and men) refusing a political consciousness in their pursuit of social acceptance.

GENDER-BENDING IN CYBERSPACE

So far in this discussion we have concentrated on the media's construction of new forms of gender identity but it's not all one-way and some women are subverting the media's prescriptions for who we *should* be through the use of new technologies such as the Internet. As we saw from the discussion of celebrity women doing it for themselves, so too are many of us performing gender in ways which make sense to us, including problematizing the very notion of gender itself. Sherry Turkle's work (1995) is often cited as the cradle of theories of gender ambiguity on the Net. Her argument that the Internet provides a context for playing with gender identity and raising gender consciousness was made as a consequence of her research with users of multiuser dungeons (MUDs), which are virtual game spaces which offer play as well as opportunities for social interaction. In her work, she found that users would choose an online identity which did not necessarily reflect anything real about themselves, including their sex.

Rheingold (1993) makes a similar point, suggesting that both relationships and identities are always suspect in cyberspace because the clues to identity which we take for granted in face-to-face interactions are unavoidably absence in the virtual world. Of course, implicit in Rheingold's assertion is the notion that interactions in real time are more authentic, unambiguous, and less open to abuse than those in cyberspace, all of which are contestable in a contemporary environment when one's true self can be masked by clever artifice. The liberation of disembodiment afforded by the Internet is usually assumed to be a transient transformation which is sloughed off when the user switches off her machine and reenters her real world. But some commentators have argued that the cyberself is not simply parked alongside the computer, ready to become reanimated when the machine is turned back on (Turkle 1995; Kendall 1998; Markham 1998). Apart from anything else, being online occurs simultaneously with being offline so that the real body is both playing at being boy/girl, gay/straight, black/white, but also eating a real sandwich or drinking a real cup of coffee. And of course, while it is absolutely true that we can perform whatever identities we want online, it is equally true that our real self is also capable of being changed through our own efforts of bodily transformation (McGerty 2000).

A persistent theme in research with women who regularly post to Internet sites is the quality of the relationships they make through their interventions and the different character of their interactions when juxtaposed with their more traditional face-to-face communications. Paradoxically, findings suggest that women can express something more authentic about themselves, articulating intimate and personal thoughts delivered through the very impersonal medium of the Internet. This is particularly the case for women who produce highly personalized mate-rial such as blogs or e-zines, as these two extracts cited in Cresser, Gunn, and Balme's study demonstrate:

> One of the best things I've found when I started using email and the Web was that I could have conversations with people that wouldn't happen if you met in person. . . . I'm in touch with all these amazing women and have formed some really intense friendships because of it . . . , but also I feel like I communicate on a different level through the Web.

> It sounds strange but I think I am the most honest within these pages than any other part of my life. I started the e-zine because I was really de-pressed after my graduation from college. I didn't know what I was going to do career-wise . . . so more and more I think I write this [e-zine] to find out who I am. Also, as a woman and as a person of color, I can say things that sometimes I wouldn't feel able to say to someone's face. (2001, 460)

One possible explanation for the candid nature of these personal posts is precisely the disembodied aspect of the Internet's communicative en-vironment where the visual cues associated with, say, making a personal and possibly embarrassing confession or statement to someone else are simply not apparent on the Internet. Both the women in the above extracts make this point in different ways, that they feel more "comfortable" revealing sensitive information when they can't see the audience for these words and, as important, the audience can't see them. Another important theme revealed in this study was the conscious and positive self-identification as "geek," "nerd," or even "misfit," where women were reflexive enough to recognize their otherness in the context of their routine life and the ways in which they could enjoy a less inhibited form of self-expression through their online writing lives. Through the telling of their own *her*stories, women online are engaged in an iterative and exploratory process of self-discovery and identity construction, often through an articulation of what they are *not*, how they do *not* conform to social expectations of normative femininity and, crucially, how they are dealing with their lack of fit with their real world..

Given the myriad ways in which identity can be hidden online, to both protect from harm but also for more sinister reasons, can a specifically shared identity for women be created in cyberspace? This is a question posed by Wendy Harcourt (1999a) a long-term feminist campaigner and critic and architect of the Women on the Net (WoN) project in the 1990s. A large part of the Internet's appeal and indeed potential for encouraging political action is its global reach, the possibility of connecting with any number of others in any number of places united in a community of common interest but where real action still takes place on real streets in real neighborhoods. Arguably, the wired woman (or cyborg woman as many cyberfeminists like to describe her) has developed an identity which breaks the biological constraint (and discrimination) of sex-based communication through the use of a piece of machinery (the computer) but also embeds it in a female-space through women-focused websites, discussion lists, and other electronic modes of communication (Minahan and Wilfram Cox 2007; Royal 2008).

CYBERFEMINISM

While so-called third-wave feminism seems to have abandoned the political project which was the driving force of both first- and second-wave feminism in favor of a postmodern, post-feminist engagement with individualistic hedonism, feminism, and feminists are nonetheless alive and well on the Web. Since the heady early days of the Internet, when William Gibson (1984) is credited with having invented the concept of cyberspace, our modern lives can now be lived, to a very large extent, online. We can cybershop, cyberbank, cybercommunicate, and have cybersex. It is not surprising, then, that we now have cyberfeminism (see Hawthorne and Klein 1999; Kember 2003; Lagesen 2008). As with "ordinary" feminism, the cyber variety has many facets, but what unites scholars and activists who labor under this banner is a recognition that, as with other aspects of social, political, cultural, and economic life, sex-based disparities prevail in the online world. Such discriminations cross-cut the digital divides which are already evident and discussed in the literature such as the divide between North and South, haves and have-nots, urban and rural, old and young, indigenous and migrant, women and men. But the very language of the Internet is gendered, women's and men's experiences of and with the Internet is often differentiated by their sex. And cyberfeminists recognize all these differences and dis-criminations and try to find ways to challenge and subvert them.

But for many, cyberfeminism is a specifically political project, in the same way that feminists don't just talk about inequality but try, through their words and their actions, to bring about actual change. However, it is an emergent philosophy and a diverse set of political practices, and is mostly manifest through women-focused websites which enjoy a huge variety of intents and interests. While some cyberfeminists such as Sadie Plant (1997) and Melanie Stewart Millar (1998) see women's involve-ment in new technologies such as the Internet as unequivocally eman-cipatory, others have emphasized the need to be critical, not just about the technology but about what women do with it, how we/they practice their (cyber)politics (Hawthorne and Klein 1999). Being part of a global network of like-minded women who all care about domestic violence or human trafficking, say, is fine, but is essentially a passive pastime if women are not, at the same time, connected into real activist networks which campaign against another lap-dancing club opening up in the town center or the closure of a women's wellness unit. "Rooting wom-en's communication experiences and ways of communicating in their social and cultural concerns and backgrounds is a principle of feminist communications" (APC 1997, 9). Similarly, Arizpe (1999) is clear that part of the challenge for feminists in cyberspace is to be active agents in harnessing the undeniable power of the technology to improve the lives of all of us, not boost the corporate coffers and maintain and strengthen the hegemony of the powerful elite. The activism-at-a-distance (Escobar 1999) afforded by the Internet, which enables those of us in the comfort zone of the West to feel good about ourselves by buying a toilet for a community in Mozambique, is, to be sure, important but does little to call attention to the tide of expired dysentery medications being pumped into the country by a cynical global pharmaceutical industry happy to make a fast dollar.

However, Youngs (1999) is optimistic about the potential of the Internet to create new ways of being and communicating between women, seeing the technology as heralding a new era of politicized feminist identity, as traditional barriers such as geography and culture are transcended by the virtuality of unreal time and space. Importantly, the Internet offers hitherto unthinkable possibilities for women from vastly different places and contexts to share thoughts, experiences, life histories and to learn from that sharing. These collective communication openings *could* constitute a radical development of strategies for feminist conscious-raising which take a global perspective and could generate global agendas for action.

As with so many *isms*, cyberfeminism refuses to be absolutely categorized, instead flirting with notions of both the post-human, woman-machine of Haraway's cyborg (Haraway 1997) and the still-human, politically active woman, using the Internet to change her world. One fundamental difference and potential conflict between these two aspects of cyberfeminism is that it is sometimes hard to see how theoretical discussions of the technoscientific cyborg figure can offer insights to the Internet's potential for women's real activism in their real communities. Attempting to weave both themes together results in the age-old problem of blending theory with practice in meaningful ways. "What happens to political action when the only politics in sight are deeply anchored in the story of the cyborg body?" (Sunden 2001, 217).

Perhaps the trick is to understand the multiplicity of cyberfeminism/s as we now understand the multifarious nature of feminism and to use those aspects which we believe are useful in explaining the social phenomena we seek to explore? If postmodern thinking has taught us anything, it is that seeking the essence of something, its inner truth, is not only a thankless task but actually unhelpful as it encourages binaries and voids imagination. So, at the same time as we acknowledge the enormous contribution which "theoretical" cyberfeminists have made to Internet research, in particular by explicating the hu(man)-machine interface and its gendered contours, we also acknowledge the ways in which actual women are appropriating this essentially male technology for their own political ends.

So we can see that cyberfeminism/s incorporate thinking about the poetics of the technoscientific woman-machine cyborg but also the regular woman in her living room e-mailing colleagues across the world with information about how to lobby their local politician. But can we imagine a virtual space in which women can both practice their politics but also explore identity beyond the stereotypical renditions of normative femininity? Nancy Paterson (1996) thinks we can, insisting that cyberfeminism is rooted in a subversive political agenda where women (may) take on the form of supercharged cybernetic bitch/goddess to challenge the male-ordered cyberfemmes which populate cyberspace. And sites such as riotgrrrls make clear both the playful and the political. As Carla Sinclair puts it so evocatively, "A grrrl site is created by a woman who addresses issues without acting like women are victims. Grrrls take responsibility for themselves—we don't blame men for anything but instead focus on ways to improve and strengthen ourselves. Grrrls enjoy their femininity and kick ass at the same time" (Sinclair cited in Sunden 2001, 222).

While such a sentiment reveals something of an antipathy toward a more overt feminist politics which, if not always positioning women as victim, would certainly see men as mostly colluding in the reinforcement of patriarchal gender relations, it can perhaps be understood as a refusal to accept that women lack agency in shaping their own futures. Is it post-ironic to speak the words of "riot" while presenting an image of thrusting female sexuality, or are women simply falling back into the trap of pleasing men with their bare breasts and bottoms? Or is it actually a double-bluff, the tough-tease-talk of the post-feminist woman using her sex to get what she wants? Who's exploiting whom, sucker? Of course, women web designers will have many and varied backgrounds and motivations to create their sites, some more clearly influenced by formal feminist politics than others. What we should be more interested in, perhaps, is less why such sites exist but rather how they support women to challenge the inequalities in their lives, improve self-esteem, and increase their sense of empowerment.

THE (A)POLITICS OF COOL

In a persuasive account of the notion of cool as a crucial component of identity, Pountain and Robins (2000) suggest that there are four elements to the construct: hedonism, narcissism, irony, and detachment. In women's identity as sexual libertine, the first two of these components are more obviously evident than the second pair, which I would argue requires a more self-conscious understanding of the constructed nature of the role being played out. On the other hand, the discourse of new-lad-speak in a magazine such as *Loaded* emphasizes both irony (although this is often a pretended humorous double-talk) and emotional detachment as ways to shore up a macho sensibility. The media's construction of the crisis of masculinity can be seen as a hostile response to the extremely modest gains of feminism, as a backlash which attempts to rescue a rugged form of muscular masculinity from the emasculating turn which is the women's movement. The other side of the flipped coin also returns women to a glorious prefeminist past where she once again likes real men, fishnet stockings, and glossy red lips, but the twenty-first century twist is that she likes to be sexy but also in control. This produces a paradox for gender relations because these new renditions of femininity and masculinity are pitched against each other, Neanderthal man vs. Super Vixen. Of course, this battle is as much a media construction as the new versions of gendered identity in play, making clear the artifice to those who want to see. These manipulations are brought into sharper relief when we consider the ways in which these updated but still normative prescriptions for gender performance are actually being subverted and transformed by "ordinary" people in both their real lives and their online activities. *Gender* and *identity* continue to be contested terms and what the postmodern turn teaches us is the joy of discarding essentialized categories of what it means to be women and men and to instead embrace the hope of fluidity and flow in our complicated lives.

FURTHER READING

Blair, K. L., Gajjalaand, R., and Tulley, C. (2008). *Webbing Cyberfeminist Practice: Communities, Pedagogies, and Social Action.* Cresskill, N.J.: Hampton Press.

Butler, J. (2004). *Undoing Gender.* New York and Oxford: Routledge.

Connell, R. W. (1995). *Masculinities.* Cambridge: Polity Press.

Harcourt, W., ed. (1999). *Women@Internet: Creating New Cultures in Cyberspace.* London and New York: Zed Books.

Markham, A. (1998). *Life Online: Researching Real Experiences in Virtual Space.* Walnut Creek, Calif.: AltaMira Press.

Pountain, D., and Robins, D. (2000). *Cool Rules: Anatomy of an Attitude.* London: Reaktion Books.

Williams, R. H., ed. (2001). *Promise Keepers and the New Masculinity: Private Lives and Public Morality.* Lanham, Md.: Lexington Books.

2

THE BODY IN QUESTION

Less than the Sum of Our Parts

A woman can't be too rich or too thin.

—Wallace Simpson, Duchess of Windsor

Are you sick and tired of being fat? Good. If you can't take one more day of self-loathing, you're ready to get skinny.

(Freedman and Barnouin 2007, introduction to *Skinny Bitch*)

If there ever *was* a time when we knew for sure what it meant to be a woman or a man, that time has long since passed and those certainties replaced by both ambiguity and anxiety. Ambiguity, because sex and gender have finally been disaggregated and there is a better understanding of the ways in which they work with and against each other, even if that understanding is often cynically employed by advertisers keen to show us their contemporary credentials (Pedersen 2002). Car advertisements which show women interested in horsepower and men interested in upholstery are intended to be ironic and play with the audience's perception of women's and men's interests. They play a game of double-bluff, on the one hand suggesting that women have technical expertise and men are in touch with their feminine side, but simultaneously implying that actually, the world isn't like that really, encouraging the knowing audience to join in the fun of pretending it is. In such cultural artifacts, gender is figured as constructed notion, but elsewhere the fixity of sex is also being destabilized with the emergence of alternative sexual identities which challenge the traditional binaries of female and male. Terms such as *metrosexual* are gaining currency among some cultural critics, giving us some hope that cracks are starting to appear in the carapace of bodily prescription. Sadly, though, these glimpses are fleeting and in the end the tantalizing promise they offer is almost entirely submerged beneath the weight of normative, sexually determined media discourse which continues to insist on stereotypical renditions of what women and men should *look* like, if not *be* like.

We are made anxious because the media's circulation of idea(l)s about what we should be, how we should perform our gender roles and our sexed selves rarely resonate well with the real lives of ordinary women and men (Bessenoff 2006; Durkin, Paxton, and Sorbello 2007). While some women *do* become prime ministers and presidents, we also know that one in four women will be victims of male, often sexualized, violence. While men might perform childcare duties, their salaries are always more than their female counterparts in almost every occupation. Most of us cannot conform to the ideal renditions of femininity and masculinity; we are not as beautiful, sexy, shapely, rich, or successful. Importantly, some of us can *never* aspire to even the most stripped-down version of the ideal woman or man because we are not white, not straight, not young, not physically able: these are attributes we can never erase, albeit some can be disguised. Nonetheless, we do what we can to get with the beat, appropriating celebrity lifestyles and downsizing their markers to make them suitable for a more mundane existence, wearing a porn star T-shirt as proxy for being Christina Aguilera or sporting a diamond stud like Bobby Brown. But why do we spend so much time feeling bad about ourselves? Why do so many of us still go along with the idea that there *is* an ideal shape/weight/size/color which, if only we could achieve it, would make us so happy? Just because . . .

This chapter is about bodies and how the media frame us as mostly a lot less than the sum of our parts, exploring the bodily discourses which circulate endlessly through popular text-based genres such as lifestyle magazines, linking gendered identities to conventional prescriptions of bodily architecture. It discusses the ways in which advertising is significantly involved in the perpetuation of particular and idealized renditions of femininity, and increasingly masculinity, working to make all but a very few of us see ourselves as constant works in progress, endlessly open to cosmetic and other kinds of bodily improvement. It goes on to consider the impact of these stylized renditions on ordinary women and men, looking specifically at discourses around both obesity and size zero as ways into understanding the preoccupation with body weight as a must-have attribute.

THE ADMAN'S DREAM

The thought of the modern world without advertising is unthinkable. From traditional outlets such as magazines, billboards, TV, movie theaters, and radio can be added more contemporary delivery mechanisms such as mobile phones and the Internet. And forms of advertising have also developed in line with shifts in technology, which have in turn changed the ways in which people get information and entertainment and thus the channels through which we are targeted as consuming subjects. The kinds of ads for any number of products which we regularly see in women's and men's magazines have been joined by viral advertising and product placement in TV and radio programs and in interactive games. Ads appear regularly on our mobile phones and are conspicuously present on websites of all kinds. If we believe the oft-quoted statistic that the average (American) citizen is exposed to three thousand ads *every day* (Kilbourne 2000), then the (potential) power of advertising to reinforce or challenge prevailing gender norms is considerable. In addition, advertising revenue underpins the economy of all but the most stringently state-controlled media, and even public broadcasters such as the BBC have a commercial arm through which it sells its products and services. Historically, public broadcasters have certainly not been averse to using product placement in programs, running the risk of sanctions from various watchdog bodies, but the lure of the advertising dollar is just too lucrative.

However, despite the considerable development of both society and technology over the past few decades, advertising content in terms of gender representation has shown itself to be remarkably stubborn in its insistence on showing (predominantly) stereotypical renditions of femininity and masculinity, women and men (see Gill 2009a). In part, this adherence to status quo bodies can be understood as a specific strategy of reinforcement, since much advertising plays precisely on the audience's understanding of gender stereotypes in order to make sense. But it is precisely the repetitive nature of these stereotypes which is so pernicious and the ways in which gender is inscribed in advertising, especially the representation of women, has been the focus of considerable academic study among feminist researchers and others for at least three decades. Gill (2007) provides a useful overview of some of the key analyses. One of the first was published in the *New York Times* in the early 1970s (Hennessee and Nicholson 1972) and showed that women were persistently framed in predominantly domestic roles and as household functionaries. Men, on the other hand, occupied almost all the authoritative roles. While this early but important study received considerable criticism because of what were seen as methodological weaknesses, the findings have been echoed by any number of studies published subsequently. Here, women's largely subservient roles, their lack of involvement in the world of work, their dependence on men, their attractiveness are all common themes in research, together with differences in stance and demeanor between women and men—the ways in which each "look" in ads. For example, men are usually taller and look down, literally, on any women who appear in the ad. Women, for their part, often look bashful toward the male figure or are positioned lying down or wrapped within a male embrace, or looking away from the audience (Goffman 1979). In addition, male voices dominate voice-overs (Livingstone and Green 1986) and women mostly talk to animals and children (Lovdal 1989; Alexander 1999; Lin 1999; Valenti 2007). When we unpack the larger category of "woman," studies show an even more depressing picture, with few instances of older women, women of color, women with "normal" shapes (that is, larger than a catwalk model), or disabled women (Plous and Neptune 1997; Ross 1997). While there have been a few exceptions to this trend in the past decade, notably Body Shop's "Ruby" window campaign and Dove's campaign for real beauty,[1] the routinized stereotyping of women in advertising is remarkably consistent over time. Despite the post-ironic turn which has inflected advertising in the same way as other cultural products of the

2000s, we now see playful ads where women know about engine size and men are interested in upholstery fabric. Such ads are noteworthy precisely because they go against the gender-traditional grain.

Women's magazines are by far the largest and most profitable of all genres within the magazine industry, and advertising for a diverse range of products makes up the largest component in most magazines, some-times masquerading as bona fide articles instead of the advertorials that they really are. Smith (1990) argues that women's magazines function as an authoritative text of femininity, where their preoccupation with changing the self to fit idealized norms of feminine bodily perfection leave readers in a perpetual state of dissatisfaction, forever seeking nirvana in the contents of a jar of wrinkle cream, through applying this hair straightener, or using that cellulite-busting massage glove. Where would advertisers be if we did not feel like this? How would slimming clubs survive? The multibillion dollar diet industry is predicated on cultivating precisely this dissatisfaction, on holding us in thrall to the lure of the perfect breast, waist, hips, and the ultimate goal, the perfect partner we so deserve. We are willingly enslaved to the prospect of our future self, seeing our bodies as sites of continuous remedial activity, forever works in progress (Winship 1987; McCracken 1993; Whelehan 2000). "Women's magazines . . . contribute to what counts as common sense about women's bodies. It seems 'normal' that women should have hairless legs and flat stomachs" (Blood 2005, 65).

WRITTEN ON THE BODY

The fixation with body shape, especially for women, is nothing new, but what history and culture shows us is that ideal forms of the female figure come and go, with fat bellies and hips being prized in some places in some periods, and eighteen-inch waists being the benchmark of ultimate femininity in other places at other times. Painters such as Rubens and Modigliani gave us images of sexy and voluptuous women, with curves and even flab on conspicuous display. Cleopatra, at less than five feet tall and with rolls of fat under her chin and a large nose, might have cut a provocative and sexy figure in ancient Rome but would be consigned to aesthetic oblivion by contemporary style gurus. And perhaps the outcome of *not* having the perfect body has been similarly catastrophic on women's health in the past as it is now, but it is clear that in the 2000s girls and women are bombarded with images of ultraskinny women who are held up as exquisite and desirable icons of female bodily perfection. That the vast majority of fashion models are at least 20 percent below their normal body weight—15 percent under is defined as anorexic according to the American Psychiatric Association (2000)—is rarely acknowledged. Can we tie the incidence of eating disorders and the routinization of cosmetic procedures for prepubescent girls—hey, get your daughter a boob job and see her life chances improve, the perfect gift for the protoadolescent—to the crazy volume of size-zero images with which we are all regularly assaulted? Women and girls (and increasingly men and boys) learn or are taught, consciously or otherwise, that appearance is a primary part of self-esteem and can be used to obtain things by attracting others and learn to see themselves as objects to be looked at and assessed on grounds of conformity to a notional ideal (body) type.

One of the major contributions of feminist scholarship toward a more nuanced understanding of gender representation in advertising has been the focus on body parts, for example, the ways in which women's bodies are often dissected in advertising: a breast, a hand, a face, a mouth (see Coward 1984). In her extensive work on women and advertising, Kilbourne (1999) argues that this fragmentation of women's bodies implies an act of violence; women are chopped up, dismembered, denied both agency and humanity as they become rather less than the sum of their body parts. These visual assaults have been picked up by others who analyze images which show women bruised, battered, and frightened and question the ethics of such portrayals as means by which to encourage consumers to buy a particular product, often a perfume (see also Bronstein 2008). The question to ask here is, what goes through the viewer's mind, flicking through a glossy magazine and seeing a woman made up to look as if she's been beaten, advertising an expensive perfume? What are the associations which the advertiser wants viewers to make with the model which will result in her or him purchasing the product? That he has a rape fantasy? That she likes it rough? As we will see in the next chapter, the pornographication of popular culture includes the advertising industry, and ads which feature overt sexuality between women and men and in particular some degree of violence are part of that trend (McNair 2002; Williamson 2003).

THE PLUS-SIZE BODY

Women's already high levels of anxiety about body shape have received a nasty boost by contemporary debates around obesity, and although much of the media's discourse doesn't target women specifically, women are nonetheless the primary focus of many health initiatives. This is not at all to suggest that obesity is *not* a major challenge facing many Western societies as evidenced by simple observation of the women and men in our local streets and shopping centers, but women are more vulnerable to accusations of obesity because it is more acceptable for men to be heavy but still be seen as in control of themselves. With women, however, excess(ive) bodyweight is linked to a lack of control over appetite, which in turn is slyly connoted with lack of control over *all* aspects of life, impacting women's life chances in employment, social acceptance, even relationship happiness. In countries like the United Kingdom and the United States, news media seem to carry reports about galloping obesity on an almost daily basis, with estimates of morbid obesity among national populations swinging a few percentage points either way depending on the findings of whichever obesity report happens to attract the media's attention. But what all agree upon is that obesity is the *big* issue of the 2000s with scaremongering among health professionals contributing to a modern moral panic that requires drastic action. Although the problem of obesity was identified, at least in the United States, as early as 1985 when a National Institutes of Health report named it as such (Brody 1985), the issue did not really become prime-time news until a few years ago. What we now see within news reports is a discourse of contradiction, blame vacillating between self, state, and McDonald's, community good balanced against individual rights. One view says that if individuals won't take responsibility for their health or the well-being of their children, then the state and public sector authorities should intervene. In Britain, childhood obesity is now regarded as child abuse and children can be taken into care on these grounds; people can now be refused medical treatment if they are over a certain weight.

But who (or indeed what) is really responsible for the increasing obesity of our citizens and therefore for slimming down our expanding waistlines? The individual or the state? As with so many other aspects of social policy, the public are more or less evenly divided between those who feel that body size is a matter of individual choice and life-style and those who believe that it is a social or physiological problem requiring a legislative and/or medical response (Stone 1997; Zernicke 2003). Schools are blamed for serving unhealthy food and stocking drinks dispensers with heavily carbonated sodas rather than juice and water. Mothers are blamed for contributing to fast-food culture as they pander to the tastes of their offspring by taking them to KFC for a treat, or packing their lunchboxes with chips and candy instead of fruit and muesli bars. The wholesome image of woman as earth mother has been replaced by mother as toxic Agent Orange, raising a generation of fatties who will die early and be a drain on state and other resources for the duration of their short, chubby lives. But occasionally, the more political aspects of fat culture are afforded a few minutes in the media's spotlight, such as Morgan Spurlock's documentary *Super Size Me* (2004), which provides a stark indictment of the commercial driv-ers which encourage us to eat more and more but enjoy less and less. Occasionally, popular media frames of obesity which mostly locate the problem as one of either individual greed or genetic propensity are set aside in favor of more complex analyses such as environmental con-cerns. As Spurlock's work amply demonstrates, the fast-food industry is, consciously or otherwise, complicit in the promotion of unhealthy diets, despite their cynical nod toward the healthy eating agenda with their new offerings of salads, fish products, and low-fat burgers. Fast-food chains have been the target of any number of lawsuits and class actions, with claimants insisting that they were not adequately warned about the dangers to their health of eating a triple-decker and fries. Most of these lawsuits are still pending, with the industry vigorously de-fending its products, ably assisted in the United States by any number of individuals with a variety of vested interests. For example, at a U.S. Senate Subcommittee hearing which met to consider bringing in a bill which would protect the food industry from lawsuits relating to obesity or weight gain, Gerard J. Musante, CEO and founder of a residential weight-loss facility, testified:

I am testifying before you today because I am concerned about the direction in which today's obesity discourse is headed. We cannot continue to blame any one industry or any one restaurant for the nation's obesity epidemic. Instead, we must work together as a nation to address this complex issue, and the first step is to put the responsibility back into the hands of individuals. (quoted in Lawrence 2004, 64)

In the United Kingdom, ambivalence seeps from research undertaken for the media watchdog OFCOM (Office of Communications), which sought to identify the links (if any) between food advertising and children's eating preferences (Livingstone 2004). While the subsequent report *does* question the multibillion dollar industry's claims that it does not try to influence food purchasing decisions by children or their parents, the report's authors were nonetheless rather cautious about suggesting a cause-effect relationship between TV advertising and product consumption. This is largely because of the complex world in which we live where precise causal factors associated with media advertising are not easily disaggregated from the array of other possible influences. However, despite this ambivalence, legislation *has* now been introduced, in the United Kingdom at least, which restricts both the volume and timing of food and drink TV advertising to children. Arguably, it has been the "School Dinners" campaign waged by TV celebrity chef Jamie Oliver which has embarrassed government into taking childhood obesity more seriously, highlighting how the media *can* be used to champion social policy issues to become part of the solution and not always part of the problem. Even though the eponymous hero's TV series was originally broadcast in 2005, his website is still up and running and still encouraging everyone to get involved: the home page features a morphed and supersized Jamie face, which conveys a potent and abidingly negative association of fat with unhealthy.[2]

To paraphrase Susie Orbach (1978), fat is *still* a feminist issue, thirty years after she said it the first time, and although the obesity debate is not always and everywhere explicitly gendered, there are any number of ways in which women are particularly targeted as responsible for the problem and therefore also the solution. The most obvious way in which obesity is gendered is in the media's framing of the culpable and irresponsible mother raising fat children on junk food, but also in the use of statistics which always show propensity for obesity to be more prevalent in women than men. In the United Kingdom, in December 2007, the latest obesity scare story centered on a report published by the Royal College of Obstetricians and Gynecologists and the National Patient Safety Agency on maternal and child health, which suggested that obesity is a growing risk factor in the deaths of women during pregnancy or childbirth. A total of 295 women died while pregnant or giving birth in the United Kingdom between 2003 and 2005 and more than half of those were either overweight or obese and more than 15 percent were *extremely* obese (Boseley 2007). Nowhere in these reports is there a discussion of the wider social and economic context which is clearly implicated, such as poor education and poverty, but rather a blame-the-victim mentality which insists that women rely on their own resources to remedy the problem, resources which are palpably already inadequate.

SIZE ZERO

In stark contrast to concerns about obesity are those that surfaced in earnest in 2006 but here focused on body shapes firmly located at the other end of the weight chart. While there has been vocal and continuing protest against the plummeting size of catwalk models and celebrities such as Victoria Beckham because of their negative role model impact on ordinary and especially young women over the past few years, it took the deaths of two models to galvanize a public debate. In August 2006, a twenty-two-year-old Uruguayan model, Luisel Ramos, died of a heart attack after not eating for several days, followed three months later by the death of Brazilian model Ana Carolina Reston who was a long-term anorexia sufferer. In early 2007, there were calls to ban young women under the age of sixteen from the catwalk during London Fashion Week in order to protect their health[3] and for all seventeen and eighteen year olds who *were* allowed to work to be chaperoned (see Campbell and Asthana, 2007). In March 2006, the British Fashion Council launched an inquiry into the health and working conditions of models, and the chair of the inquiry, Baroness Kingsmill, was quoted as saying:

During our investigations, members of the panel became increasingly concerned as we heard more details about the working conditions faced by many models and the vulnerability of young women working in an un-regulated and scarcely-monitored work environment. . . . We have been given startling medical evidence about the prevalence and impact of eat-ing disorders in certain high-risk industries.[4]

Other members of the inquiry team included designer Betty Jackson and model Erin O'Connor, who were both asked to join the inquiry so as to exert pressure on colleagues in their respective professions. While the inquiry may yet produce guidance that will help British models, the same kind of regard does not appear to extend beyond Britain's shores. Freeman (2007) argues that models who are featured during Fashion Week in New York, Milan, and Paris are *always* thinner than those working in the United Kingdom because their designers are more likely to buy into the urban myth which says that the thinner the model, the more upmarket the label.

DOES MY FACE LOOK WRINKLED IN THIS?

Of course, it's not just our bodies which need to be disciplined and dieted into submission; our faces must also be taut/taught to comply with conventional codes of acceptable beauty, which are irrevocably and forever young, white, and flawless. As Coupland (2007, 56) suggests, the ideological frame which is embedded in skin care ads incorporates the dual concerns of gender and age where ageing is seen as problematic for women and men, but where its problematic nature for men does not become so critical until later in the life. "In ads for women, consumers as young as their 20s are targeted with invocations to take responsibility for 'delaying outward signs of ageing' through regimes involving mar-ketized solutions. In ads for men, the signs of ageing are represented as appearing, and mattering, much later in the lifespan."

For both women and men, signs of ageing are both anathema—how on earth will you attract/retain a lover if you let your looks go to hell?—but happily recoverable, if only we could be persuaded to make a wise investment in an expensive face cream/repair mask/wrinkle-removal lotion, or even go under the cosmetic surgeon's knife. We know how (older) age is disdained in contemporary (Western) culture, how older people feel neglected and even vilified by the cult of youthful beauty (Healey and Ross 2002), so it is not surprising that the beauty product market is wildly lucrative. Despite the appealing idea that women should grow old gracefully and wear the badge of the "crone" as a positive and joyful emblem of wisdom and experience, such exhortations often feel shallow and even preposterous when set against the widespread experience of discrimination the thirty-five-year-old woman faces, let alone the woman who is retired and thus perceived as beyond her social and economic usefulness.

As someone who is now considered an "older" woman, having completed my half-century, I would argue that despite our knowingness, *none* of us are immune from the seductive blandishments to look years younger. I sometimes catch myself, while massaging night cream (specially formulated for "sensitive, older skin") into my face, putting my fingers under my ears and pulling the skin across my cheeks, making my eyes look weird but at least making the saggy skin and hamster pouches disappear. I idly wonder what I would look like after a face-lift even as I recognize how my own neuroses are being manipulated. It is precisely by understanding basic human psychology that ad agencies become successful, knowing which triggers will work best with which consumers. Importantly, the incorporation of scientific terminology into advertising narratives connotes a (mostly) spurious legitimacy both to the product but also our use of it: this is about health, not vanity, yeah!

SIX-PACK ABS: AN EQUAL TYRANNY?

Of course, it's not just women's faces and bodies which are disaggregated and fetishized; men too are increasingly targeted by advertisers, tantalized with the promise of ripped abs through the consumption of power drinks and a daily ab-crunch workout. Men's torsos have a starring role in grooming products which often feature a set of taut/taught stomach muscles—the largely mythical six-pack. Such bodily tyrannies are likely to provoke the same feelings of inadequacy on the part of the male audience as that produced by shapely outlines of any number of identikit women on women, but this is scarcely what most of us have in mind when we write about gender equality in the media. Portrayals of the semi-naked male body have become a much more frequent occurrence in the contemporary advertising scene, building on one of the most iconic advertising campaigns of the last century, the Levi ads featuring Nick Kaman in the launderette. The smooth looks of Kaman have almost become a beauty standard for the fashionable contemporary man, a look which somehow evinces a universal male figure through the combination of strong jaw, soft eyes, and skin which conveys both strength and tenderness (Gill 2007).

What most men's lifestyle magazines sell is a vision of hegemonic masculinity; as with their female equivalents, there is bodily perfection on show which is young, taut, beautiful, and almost exclusively white. Work with consumers of such magazines suggests that readers recognize precisely the repetitive (and unreal) nature of these images, what Connell (2000) describes as the "global" male body, even as they continue to buy the magazine and look wistfully at perfect men (Elliott and Elliott 2005). Perhaps readers tacitly acknowledge their own imperfections and hope to find redemption in the pages of men's glossies, mirroring women's emotional investment in the purchase of their own magazines and their own set of wonder products. And, as with women, men have entirely contradictory reactions to the myth of bodily perfection, at once disavowing such images on grounds of airbrushed fantasy while at the same time doing their best to attain those covetable abs and buttocks through low-fat diets, protein shakes, and weight training regimes (Labre 2005).

With a magazine like *Men's Health*, which is an internationally syndicated title selling in more than twenty countries across Europe, Australia, and Latin, South, and North America, this imagined masculinity has a global form which is more often invoked textually than in actual images since magazines are still rather nervous about making men look at pictures of other (semi-naked) men for fear of provoking reader discomfort—if I like looking, does that mean I'm gay? Women's magazines, on the other hand, have never worried about these kinds of looking relations, reflecting the very different ways in which social norms prescribe who can look at whom. It is perhaps worth noting that this reluctance to display the male body in a naked or semi-naked state has not always existed. The ancient Greeks were fascinated by men's bodies and celebrated male strength and muscularity through games (the original Olympics) and other events. However, from the mid-1800s onward, men's bodies disappeared into the closet as attention turned to the female form, and images of men were mostly produced to appeal to a gay audience, until the mid-1980s when men reemerged as sexual and sexualized subjects in popular culture (Grogan 1999). Arguably, the development of men's magazines as a specific genre can be partially explained by the dawning realization that men have money to spend on lifestyle products and might be attracted to purchase commodities if they are advertised by attractive but nonthreatening male models and/or celebrities. Interestingly, in contrast to trends which show that women's bodies have become progressively thinner over the past few decades, men's physical shape has become more muscular, showing a rather extreme form of the zero-sum game which appears to exist between women and men—the less of her, the more of him.

While products aimed at women have no problem equating beauty with femininity, when men are addressed as a target market for beauty products such as those which care for skin, there is a more ambiguous line to tread because of the potential disjunction between masculinity and narcissism (Coupland 2007). One strategy used to resolve men's potential rejection of self-care ads, even when they appear in a magazine which is specifically aimed at a male market such as *FHM*,[5] has been to use ruggedly masculine celebrities. Male consumers are thus given permission to care for their bodies by celebrity endorsement, thus allaying fears of not being "real" men (or, rather of *appearing* so by others) if they use a moisturizer or have their backs waxed. Given that many men's magazines are overly preoccupied with advice on how to have great sex (echoing their woman-oriented counterparts), men's grooming products are tied into their general appeal to women who apparently favor smooth, soft skin, and an absence of stubble, designer or otherwise.

THE RACIALLY MARKED BODY

Traditionally, most scholarship on advertising content, including in this chapter to a large extent, uses notions of woman and man as a simple analytical binary, ignoring other kinds of marked differences such as race and ethnicity, often because introducing more than one variable (i.e., gender) into the mix could make analysis more ambiguous. But the lack of more layered analyses has produced a body of critical work which, to use Dyer's (1997) analysis, sees "white" as the default race which needs no name. More recently, though, a small but growing body of work has begun to engage with multiple identities within the advertising genre (see, for example, Plous and Neptune 1997; Durham 2007), including audience-based studies with African American women consumers (Duke 2000). What is revealed in these studies is the continuing presence (or rather, mostly absence) of racially marked bodies, both women and men, which reflects long-standing cultural stereotypes about the nonwhite "other" (Wörsching 2007; Covert and Dixon 2008). A narrow repertoire of types is routinely identified, mostly focused on sex, sexuality, and sport and regular tropes incorporate aspects of the "dark side," replete with animalistic imagery, face painting, and semi-naked women in sexually provocative poses. A typical example are the ads for the liqueur *Tia Maria*, which usually show an African Caribbean woman wearing standard "jungle" clothing (ripped loin cloth, skimpy suede bra top), wild cat face painting, and a growling demeanor, all connoting sexuality and danger (Thomas and Treiber 2000). Black men, on the other hand, are often portrayed as stupid and/or comical and ads such as those for the fruit drink *Lilt* play with both these stereotypes simultaneously. Women of other colors, such as those from Asian backgrounds, play out against an entirely different set of assumptions, reflecting the stereotypes of subservience and docility which characterize Western renditions of the archetypal Asian woman (see Holden 1999).

Black men often feature in ads for sports clothing or power drinks and these products again play into the conventional stereotypes of African Caribbean and African American men as athletic and sports focused rather than engaged in more cerebral pursuits (Jackson 1994). While the *Lucozade* ads produced for a British audience which featured heptathlete Daley Thomson and footballer John Barnes have given way to Thierry Henri and Tiger Woods advertising shaving products, all these ads link African Caribbean and African American men with sport and machismo, pursuing bodily perfection and/or adrenaline-soaked recreational pursuits. As Gill (2007) points out, the use of these "respectable" black celebrity figures does provide a positive corrective to the more common media portrayals of men of color as inherently criminal; however, these more positive renditions of black masculinity still play with racially inspired stereotypes, remain narrowly confined, and rely on pre-existing notions of ethnic essentialism and difference (Rhodes 1995; Ross 1995a). Importantly, as with stereotypical renditions of ethnic difference in other media contexts, such as news or entertainment, the problem here has less to do with what is actively portrayed than with its absence. While we could argue that advertising is by its very nature *un*real, that it is mere fantasy, and that any expectation of reality is entirely misplaced, the circulation of a narrow range of ethnically marked images contributes to a cultural environment which endlessly reinforces the (racist) status quo. There *are* celebrity models of color, but they are noticeable for their rarity, with the exception of the models used in clearly marked black magazines such as *Ebony* and *Essence*. But even here, the models invariably veer toward Western norms of beauty, using women (and men) who are light-skinned and/or of mixed heritage, who have Westernized features, and who are, of course, young and beautiful. As with their white equivalents, these images of raced perfection make forms of identification with the black consumer problematic, provoking similar kinds of bodily dissatisfaction as white consumers experience when confronted by their own airbrushed perfection. The African American cultural critic bell hooks makes clear the reality of this kind of dissatisfaction for those particularly vulnerable to the media's exhortations toward idealized beauty, that is, girls and young women:

> The field of representation remains a place of struggle [and] I was painfully reminded of this fact recently when visiting friends on a once colonized island. Their little girl is just reaching that stage of preadolescent life where we become obsessed with our image. Her skin is dark. Her hair chemically straightened. Not only is she fundamentally convinced that straightened hair is more beautiful than curly, kinky, natural hair, she believes that lighter skin makes one more worthy, more valuable in the eyes of others. (hooks [1995], cited in Durham 2007, 233)

One way of reading these differences is to understand that ethnic marking serves to reinforce the notion of white as norm, black therefore as other. Global beauty norms have converged on Western ideals which privilege thin white youthful beauty over everything else. Going a little further, it could be argued that part of the process of disciplining the fat (white) body is not simply to make it conform to the beauty myth but also to stop it emulating a fleshier "black" body, the ultimate bodily transgression (Redmond 2003). Ironically, the paucity of images of black women in advertising could be seen as having beneficial effects on young black women since their relative invisibility means that there are fewer models to mimic, and therefore perhaps a reduced likelihood of young black women developing eating disorders in their quest for the perfect body.

DOES MY BOTTOM LOOK BIG IN THIS?

As with other investigations of social phenomena, determining impact and influence is an inexact science, and this imprecision, coupled with methodological differences in study design, means that different research studies deliver contradictory findings on the influence, or lack thereof, which idealized versions of the female body exert on ordinary women. Some academic criticism says that women are likely to feel dissatisfied with their bodies when they compare themselves to women they see in their favorite magazine, but how strong is that influence? Well, we can't say for sure, but what is rather less ambiguous is the trend in the incidence of eating disorders which shows a steady increase throughout the Western world in recent years, a trend which is regarded by many as a direct consequence of the valorization of the stick-thin celebrity model as the beauty standard of choice (Harrison 2000; Monro and Huon 2005). The British-based Eating Disorders Association suggests that 1.1 million people in the United Kingdom are directly affected by an eating disorder, with young people between the ages of fourteen and twenty-five being at the greatest risk (EDA 2007). The proliferation of diet plans and slimming aids, liposuction and stomach-stapling surgery, age-defying moisturizers and cellulite-busting body wraps perfectly illustrate the way in which women receive first the bad news but then the good news, damned as imperfect but then instantly redeemed because they can buy their way out of fat and ugly hell. Donna Armstrong, the editor of the women's magazine *More!*, unselfconsciously exposes the sly way in which magazines actively collude with popular media's version of the ideal woman. Describing Keeley Hazell, who was voted readers' favorite page 3 girl[6] in 2006 and who posed for a feature article for the magazine, Armstrong commented: "Keeley is a major influence to young women. She is entirely natural, not enhanced in any way. The anti-Jordan,[7] if you like. She simply has an amazingly toned body, but with huge breasts—which is what *all* our readers ultimately crave (Armstrong, cited in Duerden 2006, 8; emphasis added). As much as some of us will reject everything that is denoted by Armstrong's glib but powerful remarks, if the only women who are validated by the media are glamour and catwalk models, film and pop stars, and the wives and girlfriends of famous men, then it is scarcely surprising that ordinary young women have aspirations to be those women. A recent survey of one thousand British teenage girls aged fifteen to nineteen who are subscribers to The Lab, a mobile phone entertainment service, found that 63 percent of those who responded considered "glamour mode" to be their ideal profession (Cochrane 2005). While such a restricted sample cannot be said to adequately represent *all* young women, this finding does not seem counterintuitive but rather reflects the reality of popular culture which gives Jordan instant recognition simply on mention of her name.

However, it is important to acknowledge that not all women are forever victim to the media's dangerous predilection for showing them the skinny, digitally-enhanced girl-woman as the ideal type. For example, a number of studies, including several in the developing world, suggest that a strong sense of self-esteem is related to body confidence, which in turn predisposes women to live happily with their bodies, regardless of their shape or (non)conformity to the so-called Western ideal (Jackson et al. 1988; Lee and Lee 1996). This is not at all to argue that the morbid fascination with weight and youth is entirely a Western preoccupation, but it is to say that there is some evidence to suggest that it is probably more nurture than nature.

While some of us might dismiss the stupidity of everywoman's response to the impossible perfection of the media's idealized female form as simply uninformed, ignorant, or unconsciously apolitical, women who think of themselves as feminist (and should therefore "know better") experience conflict when considering these tyrannical representations.

In Rubin, Nemeroff, and Russo's (2004) fascinating study of feminist readings of advertising, they found that interviewees were bound in a dialectical embrace which tugged in two directions, pitting their *beliefs* against their *feelings*. Although women could very easily intellectualize the media's manipulative endeavors in attempting to corset and constrain their corporeal reality, they simultaneously worried about the inadequacies of their own bodily appearance when measured against, say, *Cosmo*'s airbrushed vision of the fabulous female. In this work, the power of the media to subvert even the strongest will is shown to be considerable. As much as I might reject *Elle*'s skinny-girl covers, I still go to the gym three times a week, telling myself these workouts are to keep fit and healthy, but acknowledging that they are also exercises in self-control. If not quite ceding the discipline and punishment described by Foucault as an exemplar of capital's victory, I *do* recognize that many of us regularly engage in an internal struggle between our politics and our practices, between our rationality and our emotion. But this is what makes us human: the acknowledgment of our own susceptibility does not undermine the potency of our arguments but rather makes them more crucial.

Interestingly, Rubin, Nemeroff, and Russo identified a useful supplementary outcome of their research in that the women who were involved in the study discovered that their own anxieties were not only shared by other women, but came to acknowledge that an interest in their appearance did not preclude them from simultaneously thinking of themselves as feminist. This revelation says much about the media's framing of "the feminist" as an ugly, hairy, man-hating harridan, as we discuss in the next chapter. While some commentators (for example, Gauntlett 2002) suggest that we don't have to worry at all about advertising's images because in a media-saturated contemporary environment which addresses us directly as knowing consumers we are far from the cultural dupes imagined even a couple of decades ago, neither are we impervious to advertising's seductive whisper. Importantly, while there are a myriad of lifestyle choices open to us, popular culture's favorite renditions of femininity and masculinity are brilliantly particularized through advertising, and even when professing irony, we still end up with mostly normative versions of women and men, as both lifestyle and identity. Even though the subtext of identity discourse is often fluid— we are sometimes this and sometimes that and sometimes something completely different—most of us do not spend a lot of time deciding who we are going to be today. We look in the mirror, we look at *Cosmo* or *Sex and the City*, and we assess how we measure up. Mostly, we fall short of the ideal and mostly this doesn't matter; we might go out and buy an anticellulite cream or a set of weights but our sense of self remains intact. But the problem is that some people *are* dramatically affected by media visions of women and men and that's why we need to take the circulation of images more seriously than simply disavowing effect on the grounds that we are all media savvy and literate, able to discern and reject the media's sophisticated pull at our emotions if not always our checking accounts.

FINALLY, A BIT OF A CHALLENGE TO THE SAME OLD, SAME OLD

In the 2000s, some retailers and advertisers began to recognize the relationship between the cult of thin and eating disorders and developed a bit of a conscience, deciding to take on board the size issue and begin to use "real women" in their product advertising. Notable forerunners were The Body Shop and the Dove brand. In 1998, U.K. branches of The Body Shop unveiled Ruby, its voluptuous version of the Barbie, in an effort to challenge the problem of the impossible body. Alongside the image of a provocatively reclining and naked Ruby in the advertising poster (a clear play on the reclining nudes so nicely observed by painters such as Rubens) was the legend: "There are 3 billion women who don't look like supermodels and only 8 who do."[8] Ruby was subsequently displayed in the stores' windows in Australia, Asia, and the United States. Mattel, who manufactures Barbie, sued The Body Shop over Ruby and insisted that the posters be withdrawn from all stores in the United States. The poster was also banned in Hong Kong on the grounds that it was licentious although posters and ads showing real women in various states of undress were allowed to remain.

The Dove brand of beauty products launched its "Campaign for Real Beauty" in 2004, using images of "real" women as an indicator that it understood the tyranny of the perfect female form and was trying to change the image of what real women are like through its conscious use of ordinary women as models in its advertising. While there was some criticism that actually all the women were within a relatively "normal" range of shapes and features—there were no extremely overweight or unattractive women, for example—the campaign *did* use nonwhite women at least and women who were not supermodel thin. The initial campaign, for a firming cream (how ironic!), was followed by a survey in 2005 of thirty-three hundred girls and women between fifteen and sixty-four years old drawn from ten countries, who were asked their views on the impact of beauty ideals on self-esteem (*Beyond Stereotypes*).[9] The findings, published on the Dove website, included the less than unexpected insights that 90 percent of respondents want to change at least one aspect of their physical appearance (with body weight ranking the highest); and 67 percent have withdrawn from activities due to feeling bad about their looks, including such routine things like giving an opinion, going to school, and seeing a doctor. The next step in the campaign is the Dove Self-Esteem Fund, developed to "make a real change in the way women and young girls perceive and embrace beauty. We want to free ourselves and the next generation from beauty stereotypes."[10] The company uses its own resources and public donations to produce educational materials to combat the impact of harmful body stereotypes and to provide support to other organizations with similar goals. Although it's difficult not to be a little cynical about these strategies—all beauty retailers have a bottom-line (in every sense) consideration and must deliver profits to their shareholders—their existence is an important indicator of the beauty industry's understanding of its involvement in promoting or damaging girls and women's psychological health.

Following on from the example set by The Body Shop and Dove's Campaign for Real Beauty, the latest retailer to develop body consciousness, at least in Britain, is the midmarket department store, John Lewis. Having already established a level of ethical credibility, the store recently issued a statement saying that it pledged to use "a range" of models to advertise its products. Having made the decision, the store then struggled to find British model agencies which could deliver "normal size" women and finally chose a South African model, Lauren Moller, in its summer 2007 swimsuit campaign (Campbell 2007). The store has also engaged the services of Susan Ringwood, chief executive of Beat (the eating disorders association), to talk to staff about responsible advertising and the use of normal size women. Whether John Lewis will set a precedent for more responsible behavior from other retailers is hard to say, but it's certainly a step in the right direction.

POST-IRONIC, POST-FEMINIST, POST-CRITICISM

One of the great triumphs of the advertising industry in the current decade is its clever insistence that the resexualization of women's bodies, especially by women themselves, is both evidence of feminist achievement but also of women's enhanced place in the world. In 2002, the poster advertising campaign for that year's Motor Show—a British event which has traditionally included copious acres of female flesh draped over very expensive cars—was on the receiving end of criticism from then minister for trade and industry, Patricia Hewitt, who declaimed the show's advertising as sexist and retrograde. However, the show's organizers insisted that the ads were "witty" and "ironic" (cited in Woolf, 2002). The ads which featured a woman in her bra saying, "The other way to a man's heart is down the M6 and off at junction 4," was not sexist but post-feminist and ironic. But really, is selling cars off the (bare) back of women ironic or just sexist and exploitative and yet another example of the same old, same old? That this particular ad was produced by a *woman* was used as evidence that Patricia Hewitt and other old fogey critics are just out of touch with the modern zeitgeist. But there continues to be considerable controversy over the sexualization of women's bodies (and, increasingly, those of men) in advertising, and simply dismissing critique because it appears old-fashioned or, more likely, challenges the boy-racer humor of male journalists is not helpful. Jackie Daley from The Marketing Store whose agency designed the ad argued, "It's part of a series intended to show the Motor Show isn't just for petrol heads but for ordinary people who like cars" (Daley cited in English and Woolcock 2002).

Al Clark, head of communications for the show's organizer, the Society of Motor Manufacturers and Traders, said many visitors to the event had found the advertisement funny. "The advert itself is quite witty and quite funny. The irony is that it was designed by a woman and it's aimed at women." (cited in Woolfe, 2002: n.p) But the question must be, what irony? Clark claimed that the advertisement reflected both the "forward-looking" and progressive attitude in the British motor industry and the theme of the show—emotional engagement with cars.

As well as these rare industry but mostly academic critiques of gender and advertising, such as the ones I hope I have made here, the other popular way of actively (as opposed to textually) fighting back against sexist advertising has been adding stickers to posters with alternative messages and/or using graffiti. Such guerrilla tactics have been extremely successful in bringing attention to some of the more blatant ads and serve as reminders that the battle for representation is far from over. Even as advertisers employ a variety of intertextual and knowing devices which attempt to subvert accusations of sexism by a specific and allegedly post-ironic narrative of disavowal, many of us are not so easily duped. The car ad slogan, "To Volvo a son" had the phrase "Better luck next time" spray painted across it. Another poster showed a woman draped across a car and had been embellished with the words, "When I'm not lying on cars, I'm a brain surgeon" (Gill 2007, 35).

FURTHER READING

Gill, R. (2007). *Gender and the Media*. Cambridge: Polity Press.

Goffman, I. (1979). *Gender Advertisements*. London: Macmillan.

Jackson, P., Stevenson, N., and Brooks, K. (2001). *Making Sense of Men's Magazines*. Cambridge: Polity Press.

Kilbourne, J. (2000). *Can't Buy My Love: How Advertising Changes the Way We Think and Feel*. New York and London: Touchstone.

Whelehan, I. (2000). *Overloaded: Popular Culture and the Future of Feminism*. London: Women's Press.

3

SEXY MEDIA

The Pornographication of Popular Culture or Just a Bit of Slap and Tickle?

> We have become so inured to sexploitation that its capacity to offend is devalued and only a handful of hard-core hairies not in on the post-feminist joke dare risk ridicule by mentioning it. (Hjul 2003, 14)

More than thirty years on from second-wave feminism, the contemporary debates around sex in/and media, and especially in popular culture, are almost the same as the early ones, with both sides as entrenched as they ever were. On the one hand are those who believe that society has become little more than a Hefneresque pornosphere with sex oozing out of every media pore, where men beat up on women as they confuse the public presentation of the endlessly available airbrushed semi-naked model with the ordinary woman on the street or in her home. The commodification of the sexualized female body, used to sell anything from cars to perfume to jeans to toilet cleaners, is seen as contributing to an increase in sexual violence against women, as the persistent circulation of such images provokes both arousal and contempt. Women pout and make themselves available to men's gaze when they pose for *Hustler*, their silicone breasts jostling for shelf space with *Period Homes* and *What Car?* as just another recreational option to pursue.

In the other corner are the anything-goes contingent who celebrate the end of sexual repression and the dirty postcard. For supporters of the so-called sexual revolution in the mediascape, the casual trade in sexually explicit material signals a wholesome and natural way of enjoying looking and doing sex, on-screen, in magazines, in the press, online, everywhere. Viva fornication! In this view, no harm is being done and wearing a T-shirt with the legend "Porn Star" is both amusing and meaningless. Sex is everywhere, not just in the places it has always been, such as films, pop videos, and advertising, but as a primary thematic on talk shows, in the subtext of *Big Brother*, and of course, spectacularly omnipresent on the Internet. Arguably, the main reason we see sex everywhere is precisely because sex sells and in a capitalist economy sex is simply another commodity to be bought and sold.

So far, so obvious. But what is missing from many of these polarized analyses is a coherent (or often any) theory of why we get what we get, other than simply restating the logic that it's the economy, stupid. Well, yes, but is there no cause and effect, no impact on us as consummate consumers? Importantly, is there no middle ground to explore between these two extremes? Even the most common sense suggests that sexualized images in popular media span a considerable range, from the straightforwardly hard-core, hard-on, pornographic through to raunchy, soft-core, erotic, and playfully sexy. But *all* these terms are endlessly contested and their meanings open to interpretation based on any number of subjective judgments. This chapter therefore aims to map the debates about sex and/in the media which have taken place over the past few decades and to explore the politics of the pornographic which animate those debates, both consciously and implicitly. It also considers some of the contemporary manifestations of our fascination with the sexually explicit, including web-based sex sites and some of the materials and products which are aimed at a specifically female audience.

PORN THEORY: THE EBB AND FLOW OF CONTENTION

Historically, there have been at least three primary approaches which have been taken on the subject of pornography and in particular the "effect" of the genre on both the consuming public but also society more generally (Attwood 2004; Evans 2008; Gill 2009b). One is the feminist, antipornography position taken up most visibly and famously by Andrea Dworkin (1979, 1987) and Catharine MacKinnon (1987), see below; another considers regulatory responses to pornography; and a third links pornography to other kinds of cultural artifact. In addition, some scholars locate issues of pornography within a wider social and political context, arguing for a more complex analysis of the phenomenon. Such analyses consider the social structures in which representation occurs as well as the content of images which are construed as pornographic and the ways in which such materials are consumed.

Historically, scholarly writing about sexual imagery and representation has tended to be framed within notions of art, erotica, and aesthetics and have been mostly celebratory and admiring in tone, possibly because most of this work has been written by men. Paying attention to the "innocent" erotic aesthetic exemplified by, say, a Rubens painting of voluptuously naked womanhood has always been paralleled by an interest in more hard-core and controversial images. However, concern about pornography and/or acceptable images and their impact began to be heard, arguably, when it became clear that the genre was moving out of the gentleman's club and onto the streets in the nineteenth century. Kendrick (1987) suggests that "pornography" is whatever the power elite says it is—and "art" similarly—and that the power to name is the power to control. Simply put, pornography began to be seen as a problem when its distribution vaulted the control of the elites and arrived on everyman and everywoman's doorstep, courtesy of printing press technology. Outwardly, in Britain at least, the debate was about the corruption of vulnerable morals by the indiscriminate consumption of "filth," but actually the real concern was women's exposure to romantic fiction and storylines which questioned women's proper place in society, a concern which culminated in the passing of the Obscene Publications Act in 1857. This anxiety was arguably the *real* obscenity—as it provoked the possibility of overthrowing patriarchy through women's emancipation—not the consumption of images of naked female flesh.

Of course, what is named as "pornography" is highly subjective, is it erotic or is it pornographic? And the answer often depends on personal preference, although in much antiporn writing so-called hard-core is regarded as the fetishized, perverted, and exploitative opposite to soft-core, which is seen as erotic, natural, and even normal. Attempts to

define precisely what pornography *is*, its contours and limits, has been a
popular endeavor but one which has never managed to achieve consensus, mostly because the images and words cannot be understood outside
of the context in which they are both created and comprehended. While
there have been, and are, legal definitions of *obscene* and any number
of prosecutions under various obscenity laws, there are some several
yards of clear blue water between what can be construed as pornography and what is obscenity under law and it mostly rests on *context*. For
example, a picture of a naked Marilyn Monroe appeared in an issue of
Life magazine in 1996. When it appeared in a calendar in the 1940s it
was banned. If it appeared today in the pages of *Hustler* it would probably be described as pornographic (Rea 2001). The picture is the same
in all three instances, but what is different is the viewing context and
the value judgment accorded to each text. Pinup calendars and soft-core
porn magazines are mostly regarded as masturbatory aids, whereas *Life*
magazine is generally regarded as a serious lifestyle publication. But the
picture is the same. Question: when is pornography not pornographic?
Answer: when the observer decides it is or is not and/or when the observer has the power to name it as such and also the power to act on
such definition.[1]

Contemporary writing about pornography, however conceptualized,
remains polarized, although some work has eschewed these mostly unhelpful binaries in order to move beyond the question about whether
pornography should be allowed to exist, to one which considers its meaning, given that it *does*. Foucault (1978), for example, theorizes that power
and cultural knowledge are always entwined and that sexuality, as both
concept and reality, should be understood within the bounds of a given
society's notion of what it is, via the discourses which arise when con-
templating the "thing." In this case sexuality, and indeed pornography,
is experienced through the conventions and rituals which have become
established over time, but which can be altered if a sufficient and com-
pelling enough challenge can be raised. Such a provocation to change
can be seen, for example, in women's appropriation of a particular set of
sexually charged images such as those available in pornography, where
a different lens is brought into play, modifying what we think we know
about the representation of women's sexuality. Porn for women, made
by women can wreak havoc with the male-ordered control over women's

bodies and indeed those of other, subordinated beings, providing an alternative if not replacement set of knowledges about our sexual selves. Women's porn does seem to offer a genuine opportunity to rethink what it means to be sexual as women in patriarchy and this is discussed in more detail later in this chapter. Interestingly, in her recuperation of the Dworkin-MacKinnon thesis, which sees pornography-as-men-as-rape, Mason-Grant (2004) makes a similar point about shifting knowledges. The difference in orientation, though, is that Mason-Grant wants us to think ourselves out of our complacency about and complicity with all things pornographic in order to confront the inherent subordination which shoots through the genre, and thus reject it. The problem with such an analysis is that it homogenizes what is a hugely diverse set of practices and materials, disavowing any potential for knowledge transformation which is about more rather than less.

THE EFFORTS OF LEGISLATORS

In the United States, the various obscenity laws enacted in the nineteenth century endured, with various amendments, for a century until the late 1980s when renewed efforts were made to rethink pornography. In the final report of the Attorney General's Commission on Pornography (1986), the antipornography position was very much to the fore, with numerous invited voices stressing that pornography was about the abuse of (male) power and that it threatened women's human rights, notably and forcefully articulated by antipornography feminists such as MacKinnon and Dworkin.

> Pornography is degrading to women. . . . It is provided primarily for the lustful pleasure of men and boys who use it to generate excitation. And it is my belief, though evidence is not easily obtained, that a small but dangerous minority will then choose to act aggressively against the nearest available female. Pornography is the theory: rape is the practice. (Final Report, 78)

Although not credited as the source of this quote, it was made by Robin Morgan, an antipornography feminist, writing in a collection of essays entitled *Take Back the Night: Women on Pornography* (Lederer 1980) and its inclusion in the Commission's Report performs three important functions. First, it shows the way in which the feminist challenge (on the antipornography side) had been thoroughly internalized by the commission's members; second, it demonstrates the ease with which the antipornography campaign slogans had become so mainstreamed as to no longer require individual accreditation; and last, it unproblematically allows to stand the assertion of a link between consuming pornography (implicitly by men) and the rape of real women as a consequence of such consumption. Arguably, the commission's findings were a foregone conclusion since such initiatives are more often about case-building than fact-finding and serve a political rather than social purpose. In addition, many of the eleven commissioners appointed were publicly supportive of the antipornography argument, the individuals asked to contribute to the review carefully chosen, and the use of evidence judicious and selective (Paletz 1988). Detractors of the report pointed to the bias of an earlier commission's findings, which argued that no evidence existed which proved pornography's harmful effects on women, suggesting that the 1986 report was biased in the other direction. The limited time frame allocated to the commission, the lack of broad-based consultation, and their superficial treatment of sexually explicit materials in terms of their cause-effect combined to produce a sense of disquiet about the rigor and balance of the commissioners' work and their subsequent report (Downs 1987). However, it should be said that in the end the report was relatively benign and equivocal in its recommendations, retreating into legalistic argument which once again subordinated clear decisions to contextual contingency.

FOUNDING MOTHERS OF THE ANTIPORNOGRAPHY MOVEMENTS

Andrea Dworkin and Catharine MacKinnon are probably the most (in)famous of a group of feminist campaigners against pornography, but there are countless others who stand behind and in front of them and who have continued to promote the arguments they put forward (see, for example, Mason-Grant 2004). In the early 1980s, Dworkin and MacKinnon drafted a feminist ordinance (law) which defined pornography as discrimination against, and sexual exploitation of, women, and thus an infringement of women's civil rights. The ordinance was subsequently passed in the cities of Minneapolis and Indianapolis in the 1980s, and the argument informing the ordinance made a serious impression on the Attorney General's Commission on Pornography discussed above. This led the commission to incorporate this (radical feminist) version of pornography into their own analysis of the impact of pornography as "harmful" to women. This is perhaps one of the few times in legal history where (one kind of) feminist politics has actually influenced government thinking, although the ordinance was subsequently found to be unconstitutional by the Supreme Court in 1986 and thrown out.

Following Kendrick, but for different reasons, MacKinnon and Dworkin's analysis is a simple one: pornography's history is one steeped in notions of power and control, about men's desire and ability to control women. From this perspective, men are programmed (either biologically or through the nurturing process) to be violent and this characteristic is an important part of what it means to be a man. "Women/men is a distinction not just of difference, but of power and powerlessness . . . [this] *is* the sex difference" (MacKinnon 1987, 123; original emphasis). In other words, relations between women and men are fundamentally about power and control, a sadly negative understanding which leaves no room for romance or intimacy. It is also an avowedly heterosexual prescription which takes no account of alternative sexualities, perhaps because same-sex abuse and rape remain invisible since to make it count would significantly complicate the much simpler notion of superior-subordinate relations founded on sex-based difference.

The antipornography feminist prescription also argues that the very act of heterosexual intercourse is itself a violent act, where a man uses his penis as a weapon: for women to say they enjoy sex and/or pornography is simply the result of false consciousness on their part as they collude with the enemy, the torturers, men. This view has often been taken as one which stands for the archetypal feminist analysis, but as Attwood (2004) points out, while it is absolutely important to interrogate images which construct sex and gender in ways which could harm women, forever positioning men as "perps" and women as "vics" closes down other readings of sexual representation. Sexual politics and pornography have

often been elided in many of the debates around sexually explicit representation so that one stands for the other. In particular, pornography has
become a cipher for patriarchy, embodying, literally, the power of men
over women, shot through with the misogyny and abuse which charac-
terizes men's dominion and exemplifies all that is wrong with sexualized
images which persistently position women as object and objectified. But
the problem with this kind of all or nothing analysis is precisely its simplistic tenor. Women are not always victim, men are not always guilty.
Women and men inhabit a world where attributes other than biological
sex and constructed gender are equally important aspects of personal
identity (to self but also to others), such as sexuality, race, age, disability. Importantly, some women like pornography and some men are
disgusted by it. These different subject positions and attitudes must be
included in any discussion about the impact of sexually explicit material
on the wider society including its potential to encourage acts of abuse
in the real world.

PORNOGRAPHY-AS-RAPE

Arguably, the continuing interest in pornography, at least by its detractors, has mostly to do with the (potential) effects of men's consumption
of pornography and subsequent abusive behavior toward women (and
children). But, as with all other research and commentary on the effects
of consuming certain types of media—violent, sadistic, pornographic,
abusive—there is no incontrovertible evidence of cause and effect because too many other variables are always present to complicate the relationship, not to mention too many entirely contradictory research findings. Philosophical approaches have been similarly tangled with some
commentators using words such as *virtue* and *flourishing* to describe the
consumption of pornography on human well-being; the argument here
being that a short-term gain in pleasure is an inherently good thing, even
if the long-term impact might be less appealing (see Kershnar 2004,
363–64). Such an approach promotes a strangely neutral stance: "Given
the unclear effects of violation pornography on long-term pleasure and
virtue, it is unclear whether violation pornography promotes or hinders

flourishing. Thus, we ought to be agnostic with regard to whether the enjoyment of violation pornography is bad for us."

No such fence-sitting posture is taken by fellow philosopher Adams (2000) who makes a very clear case against pornography, not least because if we accept that some men would rape a woman if they thought they could away with it, then the law of averages suggests that the indiscriminate availability of pornography could incite some men to commit acts of rape. In one study of rape proclivity (Malamuth 1981), 30 percent of men made this assertion and given that the incidence of rape has increased since that study was published, then men's self-reporting is likely to have increased. Using legal argument, Adams suggests that if the law protects against incitement to commit murder or racially inspired attacks, then it should similarly protect against incitement to rape, to protect the victim's basic rights. What does it say about a society which refuses to condemn the circulation of material which *could* incite men to rape women? If the case cannot be conclusively proved, surely it is better to err on the side of caution than to take the risk of harming women? But then, if we say that pornography incited a man to rape, does that absolve the man himself from taking responsibility for his action—I didn't mean to do it, but *Hustler* made me? It is precisely these kinds of competing (and sometimes reductive) arguments, about cause-effect, about motivation, about the erotic and the pornographic, which make absolute answers impossible. Despite the considerable shortcomings of the Attorney General's Commission on Pornography in the 1980s, its final report captures both the problematic nature of attempting to evidence effect but also demonstrates the seduction of ambivalence.

> What does it mean to identify a causal relationship? It means that the evidence supports the conclusion that if there were none of the material being tested, then the incidence of the consequences would be less. We live in a world of multiple causation, and to identify *a* factor as a *cause* in such a world means only that if this factor were eliminated while everything else stayed the same then the problem would at least be lessened. In most cases it is impossible to say any more than this, although to say this is to say quite a great deal. (Final Report of the Attorney General's Commission 1986, 310; original emphasis)

THE ANTICENSORSHIP ARGUMENT

One response to the MacKinnon-Dworkin assault on pornography in the 1980s was the establishment of FACT (Feminist Anti-Censorship Taskforce) by a group of feminists who were interested in protecting basic freedoms of speech and image making, although FACT did not actually champion pornography per se. Among its range of activities, FACT produced an anthology about pornography, *Caught Looking* (Ellis et al. 1992), which encouraged women to look at a range of images and read a range of texts in order to understand the complexity of what is labeled pornographic (Williams 1999). Campaigning against censorship was a guiding principle for the FACT group and other anticensorship feminists, who used the pornography debate as a vehicle through which to challenge normative understandings of the hierarchy of sexuality and sexual practices (Rubin 1984; Burstyn 1985). Often their analyses specifically engaged with and challenged the theses put forward by the antipornography crusaders, arguing against the central tenet that pornography is a process which sexually subordinates women. While there is agreement on both sides that some pornography is misogynistic and some *does* degrade women, the problem with a blanket disavowal means that one is necessarily forced back into the polarized position of offense or defense. Importantly, to deny women's desire and agency (for sex and pornography) is precisely to position her as the eternal victim and/or without sexual desire.

While MacKinnon and Dworkin made a very clear case for the prosecution by insisting on the disastrous impact of pornography on women's lives and named men as monster-architect in this process, other analyses have seen other drivers and other culprits. Foucault's *History of Sex* (1978) suggests a human preoccupation with sex and an almost insatiable curiosity in understanding its complex contours, not simply a desire for sex but a desire to seek news of sex, for the vicarious thrill of being pleasured by reports of or witnessing other people's pleasure. In addition, Foucault sees this fascination with sex to be both genuinely felt but also an orchestrated desire, a consequence of the machinery of power to compartmentalize and control even that most intimate sphere of our lives. However, Foucault's analysis is more or less gender blind and mostly fails to acknowledge the gendered aspects of desire, discipline, and control in which, in any tradition, women are rarely on top, in any sense of the word and their/our pleasure is of little or no concern. Is this because he's writing as a man? Without at all wanting to indulge in biological essentialism, men's work on sex and pornography is often rather different in character and necessarily different in perspective than that of women, albeit that as much difference exists within writings by women and men as between them.

Interestingly, many of those scholars who *have* moved the debate forward have tended to be what we might loosely describe as anti-antisex feminists, that is, feminist researchers who have self-consciously shown an interest in exploring the genre using a variety of critical tools but *without* expressing a loathing for the object of study. Attempting to find a less rigid way of understanding how sexually explicit words and pictures function in society is to recognize that the issues at stake are more than simply men's ability to exercise power over women. Yes, the power problematic is an important element of much that is described as pornography, but its contours are rather more complex than the simple gender binary which so exercised MacKinnon and Dworkin. In her groundbreaking analysis of moving-image pornography, Williams (1989) attempted to go beyond the simplistic love-it/hate-it dualism which inevitably figures the analyst as either sordid sex maniac or else keeper of society's morals. Her solution was to attempt a "neutral" tone while undertaking a scholarly examination of one of the ultimate "bad" objects, asking, importantly, what does the genre *do* and how does it do it (see also Williams 1999). One rather underresearched aspect of this complexity is that of pornography for women.

A GIRL'S OWN STORY

"Porn-for-women re-work existing conventions of explicit representation to give women a 'viewing place,' but it does so in such a way as to unsettle the normative boundaries and categories set up by existing pornographic traditions" (Schauer 2005, 48). Over the past decade, women's more conscious and unapologetic interest in things sexual, if not always pornographic, has been seen by some as a feminization of the genre. Women's *use* of pornography, as well as our interest in analyzing and

writing about it, is now mostly seen as something ordinary and visible—
as opposed to perverse and hidden—which serves to domesticate it and
render it harmless, connoting a shift from the profane to the mundane
(*pace* Juffer 1998; Smith 2007a; Wood 2008). Because the vast majority of writing about pornography has focused on an exclusively male
consumer, we know very little about sexually explicit material targeted
at women consumers or women's interest in and attitudes toward such
images and words. However, there are a few studies now emerging
which engage specifically with such relationships, and such work adds
an important dimension to the broader debates around pornography
and effect.

In her comparative analysis of websites targeted at men and women
respectively, Schauer (2005) suggests that sites aimed at heterosexual
men almost always feature men in dominant and women in subordinate
roles and focus on men's enjoyment and ejaculation (usually externally
onto the female body) either as actor or voyeur. While women's body
parts are constantly open to the exploratory and penetrative touch of
others, the browser's gaze on men's bodies is mostly oriented toward
their penis, as is the attention of the women involved in pleasuring
men on these sites. The kinds of images which are present on sites for
women, on the other hand and unsurprisingly, feature male bodies
but where the emphasis is on different parts of the body, not just the
penis. Couples in sexually explicit poses are also popular figures as are
lesbian sex shots. These latter also appear in sites aimed at men but in
the women-focused sites, the text surrounding such images suggest that
all women, despite their diverse sexual preferences, like to look at other
women, that there is an innate bisexual aspect to the sexuality of every
woman.

However, the nascent and evolving character of women's porn sites
has resulted, at least for now, in a visual and representative vocabulary
which borrows from the more established conventions of heterosexual
(male) and gay porn; they are yet to develop their own particular
feminine/feminist aesthetic, but their very existence challenges male-
defined versions of normative female (and, necessarily, male and gay)
sexuality. Importantly, they overtly address and invite the female gaze
as they target women-as-audience as their consumer base. While there
is, for sure, a profoundly progressive aspect to the development of

these sites (see especially Wood 2008), we must also acknowledge that, as with other web-based sex sites, the consumer is being courted as exactly that, a buyer of services. In other words, the positive challenge to a male-ordered world which is implied by porn sites for women needs to be balanced by an acknowledgement of the capitalist imperative which underpins any commercial enterprise, including these sassy new sites.

In Smith's work with the female consumers of the British magazine *For Women*, she argues that women's interest in images of nude male bodies has been historically ignored because the "gaze" has always been conceptualized as male, no matter the subject (2003). For women to consciously look rather than merely be the *object* of the gaze has been viewed as aberrant and deviant. However, as Smith's work shows, women do indeed like looking at nude male (and female) bodies and derive considerable pleasure from so doing, enjoying the projected fantasies which are more usually accorded to men in their own looking behavior. The magazine itself was keen to position itself "beyond" *Cosmo* in its use of explicit images and to tread a careful line between porn and mainstream women's publishing, although it was rather less successful in achieving the latter than the former. Circulation was mostly steady at around fifty thousand per month, which, for an extremely low-budget but high production value publication, was quite respectable. Its content mirrored that of men's soft-core magazines and the use of photos taken by mostly male photographers[2] meant that shots were in the familiar mode of the posed pinup rather than constituting some kind of woman-oriented aesthetic. *For Women* and similar magazines, along with other sexually focused media targeted at women, make clear that big business now understands that women are autonomous and sexual beings who are interested in purchasing such materials. Women themselves have been producing their own sexually explicit prose and still and moving images for some time but such artifacts have tended to be small scale with limited distribution. *For Women* marked a turning point inasmuch as it was produced by a national publisher and thus enjoyed the benefits of a professional production and distribution process. Although there have been other soft-core magazines aimed at women, for example *Playgirl*, these were never more than simple experiments and their life expectancy was always extremely short.

"LADIES' COMICS": A CASE STUDY OF GENTLE PORN

A very different approach to pornography for women has been taken in Japan. In her discussion of this distinctly non-Western genre, that of the Japanese comic, or *manga*, Shamoon (2004) describes the phenomenal success of what are described as "ladies comics," *redezu komikku*, in Japan. To a Western viewer, the idea of a comic being sexy never mind pornographic and/or arousing perhaps seems strange, given that comics in the West have a very specific place in our popular media diet, mostly understood as a child- and juvenile-centered genre. In Japan, on the other hand, comics are an extremely popular form of entertainment for adults as well as children and sexual imagery in all kinds of comics is routine, especially since Japan has relatively relaxed censorship laws. Part of the appeal of ladies' comics as a discrete text-based form of pornography is that they speak clearly to women's desires, constructed to resonate with Japanese women as a specific target audience. Shamoon (2004) suggests that as a genre they do this by using women's intimate knowledge of Japanese culture to produce slightly radical versions of (traditional) femininity where women take the sexual initiative, are vocally expressive in their sexual encounters, and demand pleasure from the mostly faceless men in their comic-book lives.

There are also important issues of access which work for ladies' comics so that not only are Japanese women unembarrassed about picking up a comic from a store, but they can also access the material emotionally and sexually through a particular aesthetic look and a focus on story, no matter how unbelievable, where women are the central characters and their desires and pleasures the central concern of the text (see also Juffer 1998; Smith 2007a). One of the crucial ways in which the display of women's pleasure is "evidenced"—something which is almost impossible to show in "real" moving image pornography—is through devices possible only in drawn texts, such as making clothing and even bodies transparent, so that penetration, for example, is actually "seen." Similarly, the moment of orgasm is signified by the flow of liquid, often illustrated as an explosive gush, which parallels the "money shot" of men's ejaculation but speaks clearly to women's physical experience. Interestingly, men's bodies and faces are usually obscured in these stories, although specific body parts—hand, penis, mouth—are drawn in when they make contact with women's bodies. This erasure of the male partner is part of the signature of ladies' comics and functions, arguably, to foreground women's pleasure and encourage a specifically female gaze where the appeal is to *be* the female protagonist, not to *have* her (Shamoon 2004, 94).

NETPORN.COM

Arguably, some of the most controversial sites on the World Wide Web are those focused on aspects of sex, porn sites being some of the most obvious ones in this category. As with the more traditional forms of pornographic material, two serious efforts have been made to legislate against Internet porn in the United States. The first, the Communications Decency Act (1996), was enacted but then overturned a year later on the grounds of contravening the First Amendment (freedom of speech). The second was the Online Child Protection Act (1996), which, after much campaigning, was also repealed on the same grounds in 2000, ably assisted by a 1997 Supreme Court ruling which made clear that the Internet could not be regulated because it was protected by the First Amendment. There are huge profits to be made through the sale of online sex in all its various guises, and major information and communication technologies (ICT) companies are partners in the various alliances which regularly campaign against Internet censorship (Appleyard 2000). So efforts to legislate against online pornography have been mostly unsuccessful, allowing the industry to flourish and develop ever more inventive interactive elements such as "live" sex shows, phone sex, chat rooms, and so on. The industry does, after all, earn more than Hollywood and most midrange hotel rooms around the world now offer hard-core films on a pay-per-view basis as an additional service to their guests as just another morsel to consume along with the miniature whiskey and assorted other nibbles/nipples.

The special characteristics of the Internet, particularly the privacy of being online in one's own home and not needing to feel sleazy by going out into the real world to buy magazines and videos from licensed sex shops, means that online pornography (potentially) attracts a different or perhaps an additional customer type than the ones we imagine as typical users of porn. In order to entice potential consumers further into their sites, web designers will often use free images, teasers and tasters of what's available for purchase. Often, designers make it difficult to actually exit sites through their use of repeat pop-up screens which are on a loop to try and retain the browser and encourage him or her to buy something, if only to then be allowed to escape. However, although the profits are significant and the Internet enables considerably more reality in terms of sex-based entertainment, concerns about *real* confidentiality, hacking, and security of credit card transactions have combined to produce a certain anxiety among potential browsers. So, although the much-publicized anonymity of the Internet should encourage the shedding of embarrassment about consuming online porn and safely indulging long-held fantasies, the fear of discovery by other people (through card transactions or simply being caught viewing), including by family members, also exerts a strong brake (Levine 1998).

But, self-evidently, many people put aside such concerns and enthusiastically trawl the Internet for porn. Although the Web has created an environment in which an abundance of different sites have flourished which cater to any number of weird and wonderful interests and perversions, more established parts of the porn industry have also embraced cyberspace and exploited its special characteristics to both retain existing and attract new clients. The Playboy group (for example, Playboy Enterprises), although highly profitable at the level of its monthly magazine—in the late 1990s it was selling more than three million copies each month (Spady 1999)—and its various businesses including clubs and merchandise, has been quick to develop its online presence. While former CEO Christie Hefner insisted that Playboy is a multidimensional experience which has an "intellectual, humorous and celebrity content" (www.playboy.com), the most profitable part of its online business is the Playboy store, which has thousands of items for sale in its online catalog. However, one crucial difference between the Playboy site (and lifestyle) and many other porn sites, is its emphasis on the "brains and beauty" of its models, possibly because its target audience are educated young men between eighteen and twenty-five years old. In addition, a lot of its content is free, a ploy which intends to reassure browsers that the company is not just chasing money, although the site *is* nonetheless littered with links to subscription services including to its magazine and its pay-per-visit *Cyber Club*. It is important for companies such as Playboy to maintain a loyal customer base as well as develop new markets. It therefore needs to promote itself as a respectable company which just happens to sell a tasteful line in sexually explicit material, but really, it's just good clean family fun (Frobish 2004). This is a neat trick but one which Playboy does seem to have pulled off with some success, largely because it sells a sense of community to its consumers, a community of like-minded people (men) who aspire to the Playboy lifestyle of sophisticated, man-about-town, who also happens to enjoy a little harmless porn.

Katrien Jacobs, one of the curators of the C'lick Me Festival,[3] which she describes as an exploration of the ways in which Internet pornography contributes to the development of the sexual self, argues that it is possible to move beyond the simple binary of for/against the sexually explicit to embrace a playful in-between habitus which moves beyond and between notions of heterosexuality, Western beauty, conditions of tolerance, and acceptability. In some ways, Jacobs both challenges Playboy's robustly normative rendition of hyperheterosexuality but can also be simultaneously bracketed with the bunny in her (pre) occupation of an explicitly sexual space. Her self-reported primary purpose is to extend the debate around sex and the media in order to consider the more complex questions of the importance of the erotic in everyday life, insisting that "we cannot spend all our time with cranky conversation partners" (Jacobs in Janssen and Jacobs 2007, n.p.) but should instead understand and celebrate the joy of "being naughty." She seems to be throwing down a challenge to all of us, to be not afraid of our desires, but the point at issue has perhaps less to do with what our private inner voice is saying than what the media's public megaphone is promoting. Although Jacobs proposes a "different" and more sophisticated, more twenty-first century way of considering the sexually explicit, what she ultimately argues for is a more truthful recognition of one's own *real* sexual self (Jacobs 2007). Arguably, the development of cyberporn for women is an expression of precisely what Jacobs advocates, recognizing (and attempting to respond to) desires and fantasies which are routinely rendered unsayable in a society which measures women's sexuality in strictly passive and male terms— is she sexy enough to shag?

PORN SITES AND THE FEMALE CONSUMER

Interestingly, one of the fastest growing niche audiences for online porn
are women and one (in)famous woman producer of porn films, Brittany
Andrews, suggests that women now account for 40 percent of the "adult"
Internet consumer marker (Andrews cited in Ramp 1999). While there
are different and opposing views about the power of the Internet to be a
force for good (or not), there is very little disagreement among Internet
researchers that search terms focused on aspects of sex and sexuality
generate the most hits and adult-related search queries outnumber any
other topic (Miller 2000). Estimates of revenues from these sites vary:
one report from 2002 put the value at around $1 billion per annum for
American consumers alone (National Academy of Sciences 2002) and
another put the value at $83 billion worldwide (Carnes 2002). The sheer
volume of adult sites has had an indirect effect on the kinds of research
which preoccupies Internet scholars, so there is a considerable amount
of work now available which maps the undulating contours of sex on
the Net in all its fabulous and fantastic permutations and predilections.
But what is mostly missing from this growing literature is work which
focuses specifically on women's use of sex sites and online pornography.
However, there are now a few studies emerging which do focus on
women, and it is to this modest body of work to which we now turn.

Interestingly, most research on women, sex, and the Internet (and
men's use, for that matter) is concerned with the compulsive (and therefore unhealthy) use of online sex sites, largely because the topic has particularly engaged the interest of sex therapists and/or those who write
about relationship dysfunction. For these researchers, the problem is
that the Internet allows women (in particular) to transgress the boundaries of acceptable feminine sexual behavior and their indulgence in
what Delmonico (2002) describes as "turbo-charged" cybersex leads to
problems of "addiction." The very language used in such literature, for
example, "cybersex *addict*," makes clear that value judgments are easily
made about what constitutes the normal (and therefore the abnormal)
bounds of women's sexual behavior, informed by cultural norms and traditional stereotypes (see Young 2008). So, what does cybersex actually
mean and what kinds of activities come within the ambit of this rather
vague description? Activities are often grouped into two categories,

those which are solitary pursuits and those which are interactive. In the former are included the circulation and consumption of pornographic materials (films, written texts, audio files, sex games). In the latter are e-mail exchanges, involvement in discussion groups/chatrooms, participation in virtual sex (live feeds), and communication while masturbating (Ferree 2003, 387). The specifics of sites might be heterosexual, lesbian/gay/transgendered/transsexual, child focused, sadomasochistic, animal or object related, or fantasy.

Although the Internet opens up any number of sexual possibilities and preferences for women to explore, the albeit modest research which exists suggests that women's online sexual behavior does not differ significantly from their offline practices in that women tend to prefer interactive pursuits which connect them to other people in order to form relationships, however temporary and contingent (Cooper, Delmonico, and Burg 2000). Men on the other hand seem to prefer solitary activities such as viewing pornography or playing solo games. Importantly, women's desire to be in a relationship, however briefly, rather than engage in anonymous sex, often leads them to seek real-time encounters with people they meet on the Internet, exposing them, potentially, to considerable danger. Many of us know all too well the false intimacy which the Internet fosters, as conversations with colleagues or acquaintances quickly take an overfriendly, perhaps even flirtatious, turn which takes us somewhat by surprise.

In a social context in which women still struggle for equality, the Internet provides an environment where they can be whoever they want, both socially and sexually, and thus exert a power and control which is mostly impossible in the real world. And it is precisely the blurring of the boundary between fantasy and reality which is identified as the "problem" of women's use of the Internet for sex, together with excessive amounts of time online to the (alleged) detriment of other activities, including the nurturing of their offline relationships. Most research which has looked at virtual affairs, for example, suggests that partners see such affairs as equally damaging to and a breach of trust of the real relationship as if these were embodied and physical liaisons (Gutfeld 1999). However, it is not at all clear that women are less able to distinguish between the real and the virtual and therefore at greater risk from their online sexual activities than men. Men are still more likely to be online than women and are still the primary users of sex-based sites. In some ways, such concern about women's use of online sex sites (as opposed to men's use) can be seen as just another way to discipline women's behavior by naming it aberrant or dangerous or just plain wrong. But if women prefer their online sex life to the one they share with a partner, perhaps it's the partner who is the problem rather than the Internet? If Internet sex really is ACE (anonymity, convenience, and escape, *pace* Young 1999), then perhaps we should see its impact on women's lives as (mostly) positive virtue rather than Freudian malaise. Women *do* experience inequalities in the real world, are persistently exposed to ridiculous representations of women's bodily perfection, are often subordinated in personal and sexual relations. So, embracing the opportunities which the Internet affords, which allows us to experience the pleasures of cybersex in the guise of the sexual beings we want to be (but seldom actually are), is a very modest form of kickback.

The other way in which women are using the Internet to subvert the patriarchal hegemony of the contemporary social, cultural, and economic environment is by becoming developers and not just consumers of Internet services, including getting involved in the construction of cybersex sites. In an interesting study of owners and producers of sex-based sites, Podlas (2000) found that thirty-five (of seventy-one sites in the study) had women as owner-producers and all but one of these women were key performers in/on their sites. Only thirteen (out of thirty-two) of the men who were owner-producers featured prominently on their sites. When asked, women did not see their activity as antithetical to women's empowerment or demeaning to women but rather saw themselves providing alternative ways of imagining the relationship between women, sex, and the Internet, including offering different models of representation (of women and sex) and control. Many of the women who took part in Podlas's study had previously worked in the sex industry and switched to the Internet because of the control, flexibility, and better working conditions (including safety) it offered, especially when compared with the traditional industry, which is male-dominated and mostly poor paying for anyone other than the owners. Women's ownership and control of cyberporn sites can, potentially at least, shift the contours of women's sexual representation beyond the narrow imagination of men:

Pornography is, presently, a tool of men, defining women and resulting in their subjugation and objectification. The Internet is also a tool created by men. Nonetheless, with these tools now in the hands of women, they can be used to dismantle the master's house. In this way, as cyberporn entrepreneurs, women can truly be mistresses of their domain. (Podlas 2000, 853)

JUMPING THE LIGHT FANTASTIC: THE PORNOSPHERE AS LIBERATION *AND* EXPLOITATION

While Podlas's breezy optimism for the opportunities afforded to women's career progression by the cybersex industry is perhaps a little overstated, the general trend she describes *does* suggest that the dangers to women of sex-on-the-Net are not ubiquitous and that women *can* be significant beneficiaries of the Internet's bounty when they take control of the technology and make it work for them. But such positives need to be mapped against some of the less attractive aspects of our sex-saturated media world, especially the management of our sexual selves. Without wanting to retreat into simplistic notions of false consciousness, a large question mark hangs over the performance of women's give-it-to-me sexuality in terms of push and pull. In other words, do women perform sex according to an authentic sense of self-empowerment—at last, I can be the sex siren I've always wanted to be—or because this is what the media dictates, thrusting cleavage as the new cool? Without wanting to suggest that always and everywhere women are the latest cultural dupes (following Fiske, 1989), pressure to conform, especially for younger women and especially when that conformity is actually quite fun and actually rather sexy, *is* seductive and hard to deny. But let's at least recognize what's going on so that we buy our Playboy T-shirt consciously *knowing* that, no matter our reason for doing so, we are pretending our way into the porn-star lifestyle because that's the must-have look dictated by something or someone other than ourselves.

Understanding our sex-fixated culture as merely the latest manifestation of capital's clever game plan is to apprehend precisely the power of money to define style, define identity, define how we should perform our sexual selves. In her inventive analysis of the sex toy industry, Smith

(2007b) suggests that sex accessories have finally moved out of the dark of the licensed sex shop and into the bright light of the coffee table in an exuberant display of form over function. The rise of designer sex shops such as Coco de Mer and Myla signals what Smith describes as the "poshing up" of sex: addressing the sexual desires of women translates into an act of public service as adult shops which specifically target women move into the respectable public space of the shopping mall. Licensed sex shops on the other hand continue to inhabit a murky half-life with their blacked out windows, private signage, and almost exclusively male clientele. The public-private habitus of stores catering to women and men respectively thus turns the more conventional women-private/male-public dichotomy on its head and perfectly exemplifies the recasting of sex as simply another facet of domestic labor. The peephole bra gets written in below the marinated tuna steaks as just another supper treat on the shopping list of today's modern woman. In the end, we are always first a consumer and only after that primary definition do we claim (are allowed?) any other kind of identity, sexual or otherwise.

At the beginning of this chapter, I questioned whether the pornosphere is a force for good (sexual liberation as twenty-first-century nirvana) or ill (continuous incitement to perpetrate sexual harm against women). Where this chapter ends is by arguing that polarizing the debate about sexymedia does not get us very far, not only because life is more complicated than that but also because what "counts" as pornography is highly contested. One person's empowerment is another's repression: my erotica is your porn.[4] The representation of sex in popular culture cannot therefore be simply dismissed as always and everywhere pornographic, phallocentric, and misogynistic, made by men for men's pleasure, forever exploiting women, both actually and ideologically. For sure, some texts and images *are* those things but the proliferation of sexually explicit material aimed at a couples market, or made by and for women, or by and for lesbians or gay men problematizes simplistic arguments about cause and effect. But nor is it right to say, incontrovertibly, that there is *no* effect because we simply cannot know that for certain, and in any case, such a perspective rather goes against our intuitive sense that advertisers spend billions of dollars every year for a reason.

The other fundamental issue we have to recognize is the commercial imperative which underpins the development of contemporary culture's promotion of the sexually explicit as consciously cool, which again brings us full circle. Conspicuous consumption of a sexy identity and lifestyle as with anything else, takes time, energy, and cash and for as long as new products are coming onto the market and popular celebrities are endorsing them (or even producing them, witness the avalanche of celebrity perfumes cascading into department stores), sex-soaked culture looks like being around for a while yet. And those of us who question, however gently, a business practice which trades women's bodies as just another commodity feature do so at our own risk. Being cool is good and dissent is cast as unfashionable spoilsport talk. But thank goodness some of us are willing to poke our heads above the parapet and ask if wearing "Fit Chick Unbelievable Knockers" across our breasts really *is* the ultimate sign of women's liberation in the twenty-first century.

> We've become a heavily sexualised culture, but it's consumerism and sex rolled into one. Revolutionary movements tend to be co-opted—swallowed up by the mainstream and turned into pop culture. It's a way of neutralizing it . . . it makes it all safe and palatable, it shuts up the radicals. Once that happens, the real power is pretty much dissipated. (Candida Royalle[5] quoted in Levy 2005, 196)

FURTHER READING

Attwood, F. (2004). Pornography and objectification. *Feminist Media Studies* 4(1): 7–19.

Dworkin, A. (1979). *Pornography: Men Possessing Women*. New York: Perigee Books.

Jacobs, K. (2007). *Netporn: DIY WebCulture and Sexual Politics*. Lanham, Md.: Rowman & Littlefield.

Levy, Ariel. (2005). *Female Chauvinist Pigs: Women and the Rise of Raunch Culture*. London: Pocket Books.

Mason-Grant, J. (2004). *Pornography Embodied: From Speech to Sexual Practice*. Oxford: Rowman & Littlefield.

MacKinnon, C. (1987). *Feminism Unmodified: Discourses on Life and Law*. Cambridge, Mass.: Harvard University Press.

Williams, L., ed. (2004). *Porn Studies*. Durham, N.C.: Duke University Press.

WOMEN IN/AND NEWS

The Invisible and the Profane

It was, as is so often the case, reading *The Guardian* that did it. There was page after page, 15 of them, yesterday morning, of men writing about men: not a single female byline, nor a single prominent female photograph (there was a tiny one of Dame Eliza Manningham-Buller), in the whole of the home news pages. Barely a woman in sight till I got to Polly Toynbee. There were male suicide bombers, and their male barristers and a male judge and male home affairs spokesmen, and there were broadcasters—not one woman among the long list of Sony radio award winners—and there were fat politicians, and all these men writing about what all these other men were doing.

—Alice Miles (*Times*, May 2, 2007)

As we approach the end of the first decade of the new millennium, and I realize that I have been researching the relationship between gender and news for fifteen years and the conclusions I came to in 1994 are remarkably similar to those I would make today, I feel sadly depressed. Even though more women than men enroll in journalism courses, are entering the media industry in unprecedented numbers, are an increasing presence as middle rank if not always the most senior staff in newsrooms, what we see, read, and hear is mostly news about men. "Where are the women?" is a horribly familiar question which appears in numerous research studies which deconstruct news discourse and investigate gendered relations in the newsroom. This is not to say that absolutely nothing has changed over the past few decades or so, because there *have* been some significant gains, mostly won as a result of fearless campaigning by women (and some men) within the news industry (see Byerly and Ross 2006). But these shifts have been slow and painfully wrought, often at the expense of women's careers within mainstream news (de Bruin and Ross 2004; Robinson 2005; Ross 2005). This chapter thus looks at this question in more depth, first by outlining some basic ideas about the constructed nature of news and the ways in which journalists, either wittingly or otherwise, persistently use a narrow range of "frames" which stereotype women. It then considers some of the historical research conducted about women and news, showing the ways in which over time and across continents, women are rendered almost invisible in mainstream news discourse and that when they *do* appear are seldom granted autonomy but instead are more usually framed as victims, trophy wives, or girlfriends.[1] As both elites (e.g., politicians) and as ordinary people (e.g., members of the public), women's voices are mostly silenced, leaving the business of bringing and actually *being* the news of the world to men, albeit with the exception of a few women journalists working in news. Specific analyses of three sets of relationships then follow which focus on women in politics and media, women as sources in news articles, and women as newsworkers. I suggest that much of what we see, hear, and read about in mainstream news is a result of a newsroom culture which continuously reproduces itself. This culture is not specific to particular national contexts but rather has been revealed as operating in many different global environments, manifesting as a repressive structure of newsthink which locks its practitioners (both women and men) into stereotypical modes of reporting which masquerade as "neutral" news values, but which perpetuate a male-ordered environment which is often hostile to women (Opoku-Mensah 2004; Melin-Higgins 2004; Robinson 2005; Geertsema, 2009).

DECONSTRUCTING NEWS

The perpetuation of a hegemonic worldview of male dominance is regularly witnessed in both fiction and fact-based media and the ways in which women (particularly but also other disadvantaged groups) are represented in the media send important messages to the public about women's place, women's roles, and women's lives. If it has become commonplace to argue that news media regularly and routinely perform an affirmatory function in reinforcing dominant norms and values to the public, it still bears repeating. The sadness and frustration is that after several decades of documenting the media's representation of women in news (see for example Tuchman et al. 1978; Root 1986; Ross and Sreberny-Mohammadi 1997; Wykes 1998) so little has changed. This is absolutely *not* to undermine the efforts of women (and men) over the past decades who have worked assiduously toward the goal of greater equality. But it *is* to argue that the stereotypes of women which emerged from scholarship such as Gaye Tuchman et al.'s foundational work on images of women in mass media (1978) and Jane Root's (1986) work on women and television are almost exactly the same ones which feminist media scholarship identifies in the contemporary context of the early twenty-first century. Importantly, part of the endurance of gender stereotypes in news discourse can be related directly to the culture of newsrooms themselves, microcosmic environments which constitute sites of considerable contestation about gender and power (Steiner 1998; Gallagher 2001; de Bruin and Ross 2004; Robinson 2005). So, despite a global women's media movement that has lasted more than three decades and made gains on both legal and cultural fronts in most nations of the world, sexist media representations have endured. The underground nature of pornography industries has now leached into the mainstream of many nations, with violent videos (featuring abuse and denigration of women) now available in the corner video store and billboard advertisements parading nude and near-nude figures of both women and men, as we saw in the previous chapter. Television programming in some nations—particularly when scheduled in the late night zone—feature overtly sexual content, including graphic sexual assaults (Levy 2005). Print and television news are similarly problematic, especially as they have shifted toward celebrity and "lighter" content.

Although it is possible to think that the ways in which women are constructed and represented in entertainment genres are mere fantasy and don't necessarily say much about women's place in the real world, the same comforting thought cannot be brought into play when considering women and/in news discourse. While program directors and filmmakers might insist they must be free to follow their creative muse wherever it takes them, even if that's into politically incorrect waters, news media workers on the other hand insist that what they show us is indeed the *real* world. The lie of authenticity which sits behind this facile and pompous claim has been constantly challenged by any number of studies which seek to understand how news *really* works, how decisions about content are made, how sources are identified and used, who owns the media, and so on (Tunstall 1977; Jones 1996; Franklin 1997, 2006; Croteau and Hoynes 2001; Manning 2001; Cottle 2003a, 2003b, 2004; Sanders 2003; Hesmondhalgh 2006; McNair 2006). That news programs prescribe their own routinized functions and protocols in the same way that fictional formats have *their* own internal logics—for example, soaps need dramatic tension, changing relationships, disasters, and so on—is often not appreciated by the audiences for news. There is never any acknowledgement that what we see, read, and listen to in the news is the result of myriad selection decisions which follow so-called journalistic conventions in terms of what constitutes a "good" news story (see Allan 2004). But news programs are deeply contradictory in nature: on the one hand they provide a regular update, at the macro level, on the social, political, economic, and cultural order of the day (Bennett 1997). Thus news media perform an affirmatory and confirmatory function in (re)articulating the rules of the game to which we are all supposed to subscribe. But then, on the other hand, news comes to us, the audience, in small, discrete units which are often free-floating in a contextual vacuum, lacking background and thus unable to offer us precisely the explanatory coherence which would enable sense to be made of the particular news event in question (Iyengar 1991). News stories are everything and nothing at once, providing "information" about the social world but often without the necessary context which would make the events described fully meaningful. In other words, we get information but not necessarily knowledge.

As Norris (2004) argues, to understand news it is first necessary to understand the various frames within which news narratives are contextualized (see also Entman 2007). These frames provide an interpretative structure which enables a particular story to be described but they are not value-free. They are, rather, ritualized ways of understanding the world, of presenting a reality which excludes/includes, emphasizes/plays down certain facts. News frames constitute highly orchestrated ways of making sense of social (including gendered) relations which encourage a commitment to share a particular interpretation of and ways of seeing the world which are entirely partial and preserve the male-ordered status quo. News media and in particular television, with its huge audience share, are arguably the primary definers and shapers of the news agenda and perform a crucial cultural function in their gendered framing of public issues and in the gendered discourses they persistently promote. If news media fail to report the views of women judges or women parliamentarians or women business leaders but *always* report on violent crimes against women, then it is hardly surprising that the public fail to realize that women do occupy significant roles in society or, equally, that men are much more likely to be victims of serious crime than women.

GENDER IN THE FRAME

Over the past decade, successive studies have attempted to map and analyze the ways in which women are portrayed in factual media and that *her*story is not especially positive, showing as it does a pattern of marginal presence on the one hand and stereotyping on the other. For example, in 1995, the Global Media Monitoring Project (GMMP) was established to coordinate a simultaneous monitoring of news media on one day across seventy-one countries in order to explore patterns of gender representation in news. In that study, it was discovered that globally 19 percent of individuals who featured in news stories were women and that their most popular representations were as victims, mothers, and wives (MediaWatch 1995). Five years later, a follow-up monitoring exercise undertaken with more or less the same number of countries and which included the analysis of fifty thousand–plus separate news items found that the focus of women-oriented stories was almost identical to the previous study and that the proportion of women featured in news stories had actually gone down by 1 percent (WACC 2000). Once again, the "woman-as-victim" trope was the most popular. In both those studies, radio, TV, and the press were monitored nationally, regionally, and locally but there were few points of difference across these different parts of the news landscape. The third monitoring exercise, in 2005, showed a very slight improvement, with the proportion of women featuring in news items rising to 21 percent but where the categories of representation were almost identical to the findings of the two previous studies.[2]

Looking at the European scene, the European Commission (1999) conducted a pan-European analysis of gender and news representation and the rather negative conclusion of the report cited a low volume of women's appearances in the media across all genres and argued that women were overrepresented as victims, usually of violence, often sexual in nature. In a Scandinavian study in the mid-1990s, researchers found that women in the national news media were often subject to overly sensational reporting (NOS 1995; Michielsens 1991) and later British studies provide yet further corroboration (see Carter and Weaver 2003; Kitzinger 2004) of this trend. The European Commission's study also found that "old" forms of gender stereotype had recently been (re-)introduced as a consequence of political and economic upheaval, so that German reunification had resulted in a new emphasis on women as mothers and housewives. In former Eastern European countries, demands for Western goods and services including easy sex have encouraged the reemergence of women as sex objects in popular media discourse in those already ravaged and now ravished countries (Lemish 2004).The commission's gloomy conclusion was that "the most that can be said is that change in gender images is hesitant and contingent" (European Commission 1999, 13).

On a different continent entirely, a study of twelve countries in Southern Africa—the Gender and Media Baseline Study—was undertaken in 2003 using the GMMP model.[3] That study found that women are "grossly under-represented and misrepresented both in the newsrooms and editorial content of Southern Africa [and that] there are still cases of blatantly sexist reporting that portrays women as objects and temptresses." (Genderlinks, 2003: 12)[4] In the Middle East, in her work on Israeli media's portrayal of Russian women immigrants, Lemish (2000) comes to similar conclusions, arguing that the "whore" motif was the one most frequently used. Of course, there are always exceptions to every rule and a surprising example of this can be found in Fahmy's analysis of Associated Press photographs in the period during and after the Taliban regime in Afghanistan (2004). In her work, Fahmy suggests that although there were enduring frames of women's subordination, most women in the sample were portrayed as interactive, involved and symbolically equal to the viewer when considering photographic features such as point of view, social distance, and imaginary contact. She concludes that AP photographers appear to be reflecting the realities of a more complex set of social relations, as some women wear the burqua and stay in sex-segregated environments while others simultaneously perform liberation in the context of a deeply traditional society with their high-powered jobs and sometimes senior political positions.

WOMEN AS VICTIM: THE TROPE OF FEAR

As discussed above, one of the most frequent frames of women in news discourse is as victim and the media's fascination with the fragile female form and her vulnerability to violation probably bears a little further scrutiny since it says something very powerful about women's agency and women's role in society. Several studies which have used qualitative approaches to researching women and news have looked at the media's treatment of women and violence, and in particular, the media's reporting of sex crimes (Soothill and Walby 1991; Kitzinger 1992, 2004; Lees 1995; Cuklanz 1996; Korn and Efrat 2004: Mason and Monckton-Smith 2008). Women who are the target of male violence are routinely described as "victims," placing them as eternally passive and dependent, their lives entirely circumscribed by the whim of men. Of course, women *are* victims in such situations, but most are also survivors, but these "after" stories are rarely covered as the media moves on to report the next salacious assault. Identikit pictures of assailants are captioned with "sex monster," "crazed animal," or "fiend" labels, which distance these men from the ordinary variety, implying that normal men do not do these things, only beasts and maniacs do. In Britain, the law was changed in 1993 in order for a young man under the age of fourteen to be convicted of rape, and at the time the media carried reports that suggested "the public" was concerned at "moves which could put more young children behind bars" (*Guardian*, December 11, 1994; emphasis added). The use of the term *children* here makes a clear value judgment, that an adolescent male who commits an act of rape is childlike in his inability to distinguish right from wrong.

The framing of sexual assaults as "unusual occurrences" carried out by "unnatural men" encourages the view that such crimes are both rare and the result of individual pathology requiring a law and order response rather than constituting a serious social problem requiring a social reform solution. And the fast turnaround for news in the contemporary just-in-time newsroom environment, as well as a lack of interest in providing context for any story, means that each time a rape case is reported, it is as if for the first time. This results, once again, in the framing of such items as isolated and random events rather than the consequence of patriarchal power relations that structure *all* personal relations, including sexual ones (Myers 1997; Berns 1999; Cuklanz 2000; Mason and Monckton-Smith 2008). But using the frame of rapist-as-sex-fiend flies in the face of the considerable evidence from even a cursory look at sex crime statistics all over the world, which shows that the majority of convicted rapists are friends or acquaintances of the (mostly) women they attack. So why does the orientation and language of most news reports on sexual violence still perpetuate the "sex beast" or "stranger-danger" myths, despite the facts relating to intimately acquainted violence? One might speculate that one reason could be that to acknowledge that hard and shocking reality is to acknowledge the very thin line that separates the thought from the act, the shouting from the slapping, the tongue from the knife, them from us.

Benedict's (1992) study of sex crime reporting found that women were often blamed for their "provocative" behavior but that not all victims were framed in exactly the same way. White, middle-class women tended to get more favorable coverage than either black women or working-class women. Thus, as with other kinds of crime reporting, issues of gender are further complicated by issues of race, echoed in more recent work by Meyers (2004) and Wilcox (2005). Exactly the same kinds of value judgments are, of course, also made about the perpetrator, so that the good husband must have been provoked but the social isolate is truly monstrous. Mostly, the media message is clear: men just can't help their biological urges and women must dress modestly if they are to avoid provoking a sexual assault. It is thus women who have to bear the burden, in every sense of the word, of men's inadequacies, women who must modify and change their behaviors, women who carry guilt in their DNA. In media terms, women appear to be at their most interesting when they are in the most pain, when they experience most suffering. Vetten (1998, 8), at the Center for the Study of Violence and Reconciliation in South Africa, argues that "as a general point, of course men accused of rape are entitled to present their version of events, as are the women concerned. But when women are not given this opportunity, then coverage of rape rapidly degenerates into a media trial by innuendo and speculation." But the ways in which rape cases are dealt with by the media are not always the same and the contradictory rhetoric surrounding particular incidents could as easily encourage as discourage more women to come forward to report a sexual assault. Using the example of Nombonis Gasa who was raped in 1997 on Robben Island, Vetten (1998, 5) suggests that

> the assault was widely and schizophrenically reported on, with Ms. Gasa being portrayed at various times as a liar, a survivor/heroine, an indulged government favorite, or MP Raymond Suttner's wife. One Afrikaans newspaper, along with some members of the SAPS [South African Police Service] denounced Ms. Gasa as a liar who concocted a false rape allegation; simultaneously, *Femina* [a woman's] magazine, honored her as a woman of courage.

The contradictory approaches which journalists use to report on sex crimes continue to inform the tense debate over the precise role that the media plays in, on the one hand, trivializing sexual violence against women and routinely discrediting women's testimony, and on the other, helping to highlight what has become an almost endemic problem and thus encouraging more women to report such crimes to the police. Of course, as Vetten and others have pointed out, the media often do both simultaneously.

PORTRAITS OF ELITE WOMEN I: WOMEN PARLIAMENTARIANS IN THE EVERYDAY[5]

While women-as-victim stories are by far the most frequent type of gender-framing in mainstream news, the slow but steady progress of women decision makers, as parliamentarians, local council members, CEOs, and other senior professional women has prompted an interest in studying the ways in which such elite women are portrayed in news media, especially politicians (Liran-Alper 1994; Fowler 1995; Kahn and Goldenberg 1997; Norris 1997b: Lemish and Drob 2002; Ross 2002; At-keson 2009). In all these studies, a primary argument is that women parliamentarians are rarely treated by the media in the same way as their male counterparts; they are always rather less than the sum of their body parts. They are persistently trivialized by media speculation over their private lives, domestic arrangements, and sartorial style: they might be allowed to speak about policy, but their potency as change agents or even as serious politicians is casually undermined by the media's use of extraneous detail such as their age, where they buy their shoes, and which stylist they use.

In a modern democracy such as that fondly imagined to exist in the so-called civilized West in the twenty-first century, most journalists would say that they write and broadcast in the public interest, that they serve an important function in holding government accountable and reporting on the actions of those whom we elect to serve in our name. But as news media move ever further and faster toward providing mere infotainment, so their ability or even interest in reporting politics in any meaningful way goes at equal velocity in the opposite direction. And while the rhetoric of impartiality, which the news media have always insisted lies at the heart of their practice, has never been as pristine as journalists have claimed, the line between journalist and politician has become increasingly blurred. Obviously, for both sets of professional actors, there is a necessary interdependence, since journalists need something to write about and politicians need to get their messages across to the public. Because of the media's belief that the public have an alarmingly short attention span, they tend to apply sound bite theory to both political interviews but also to what they choose to cover. This results in a rather distorted view of the political process, at least from the general public's view. Politicians themselves are very well aware of the news media's need to make news exciting, as the Labor politician Jenny Macklin makes clear.

The problem with the electronic media is, you know, it's only 10 seconds which is of course, going to come out of *Question Time*, because it's the only color and movement of the day. The rest is the 'normal' process of making laws, committees and there are a lot of positive things that go on but you wouldn't put it on the telly at night because it's as boring as anything. (Jenny Macklin, Labor, Australia)

Talking about Ourselves

When asked, women politicians themselves are clear that a specifically gendered news discourse *does* exist when journalists report on the political activities of women and routinely frame them as women first and then, maybe, as politicians. When 101 Labour women were elected to the British Parliament in 1997, the front-page headlines figured them as "Blair's Babes." Although some of those women have argued in retrospect, that doing the "Babes" picture was perhaps unwise, they were unprepared for the media response: their considerable victory was trivialized instantly not just by that possessive apostrophe, but through their sexualized figuring as babes. The reality is that women *have* been elected to the top political job, have been and are presidents and prime ministers, but still their ability to lead their country is questioned, still the media ask, can they really do it? Two contemporary examples of this phenomenon are the election of Angela Merkel in Germany in 2005 and the promotion of Margaret Beckett in the United Kingdom to Foreign Minister in 2006, two resounding firsts for women in those respective countries. In each case, the woman in question had many, many years of active political office but still the media questioned their competence and suitability for the job.

Another problem for the campaign, however, was Merkel herself. Despite the orange posters and the theme song Angie from the Rolling Stones, there was not much rock 'n' roll in the Merkel camp. Its flag-bearer was mocked as a frumpish former academic unable to connect with ordinary people. (Matthew Campbell Templin, *Sunday Times*, September 17, 2005)

The appointment of Mrs. Beckett displays another variety of his [Tony Blair] contempt for the significance of high office. . . . Following her record of success in government—the most recent evidence of which has been her attempt to destroy agriculture by fouling up the system of payments to farmers—she is lucky to be left in charge of so much as a sweet shop. (Simon Heffer, *Daily Telegraph*, May 6, 2006)

Arguably, the media's reaction and response to women who dare to cross the gender line and do "men's work" is to punish them, as if women's success must be at the expense of men, the ultimate zero-sum gain played out on the laptops of male journalists. Women parliamentarians themselves argue that the media often appear to be operating double standards when considering women politicians, that they expect better standards of behavior, higher moral values, more honesty, integrity, and loyalty. Women are often set up as paragons and then unmasked, almost as quickly, for being less than perfect, but they never claimed such perfection, the media made it up!

> Women politicians, particularly at cabinet level, tend to be knocked, judged, assessed, by criteria that are incredibly harsh, relative to their male counterparts. . . . It's not that the media wouldn't want to focus on men when mistakes are made but it is more relentless with women, it's personalized in a way that it isn't with men. (Janet Love, ANC, South Africa)

Where Did She Get Those Shoes?

News stories about powerful women are just as likely to use frames of analysis which privilege biology rather than competence and most of them believe that their outward *appearance* is the focus of both more column inches and airtime than anything they might *say*. Fiona Mactaggart (Labour, U.K.) believes that the media's fascination with sartorial style is partly because there is a view that how women dress is a much more important indicator of who they are and what they stand for than is the case for men. The emphasis on style functions to undermine women; it is *not* an *un*conscious process. In an interesting poacher-turned-gatekeeper analysis, the Women in Journalism group[6] undertook a study of newspaper photographs which revealed that although it is clear that "men outnumber women in public life . . . the analysis shows that the way newspapers use images of women is at best old-fashioned and at worst complacent" (Women in Journalism 1999, 12). "Women are never the right age. We're too young, we're too old. We're too thin, we're too fat. We wear too much make-up, we don't wear enough. We're too flashy in our dress, we don't take enough care. There isn't a thing we can do that's right" (Dawn Primarolo, Labour, U.K.).

When Cheryl Kernot crossed the floor of the Australian Parliament in 1997, giving up her leadership of the Australian Democrats to become a Labor candidate, the media responded, in picture form, with cartoons of her in bed with Kim Beasley (then Labor party leader). While men are also the subject of the cartoonist's wit, women are much more likely to feature in cartoons which emphasize aspects of their sex and sexuality. A woman politician is always described as a *woman* politician; her sex is always on display, always the primary descriptor. She is defined by what she is *not,* that is, she is not a typical politician who allegedly bears no gendered descriptor but who is clearly marked as *male.* If elections are won or lost in the public gaze of the media, as the media itself has often claimed, then it is easy to argue that the privileging of form over function, presentation over policy, means that *all* politicians are subject to the tyranny of telegenity and must surrender to persistent sartorial scrutiny, not just the women. While this is, in principle, true, the objectification of male politicians is noticeable because of its infrequency. With women politicians on the other hand, it is almost de rigueur.

Norris (1997a) argues that a number of frames exist that position emergent women leaders as breaking the mold, as outsiders winning against the odds, and as agents of change. These are all very positive frames at a superficial level but the first two at least are unsustainable over the lifetime of a woman leader's career, once she is an established rather than a new leader. The third frame is equally problematic since it could, by its emphasis on change (challenging the barren desert of politics as usual), set women up to fail as they prove unable to achieve the unrealistically high expectations the media have of them. Beyond the obsession with the physicality of women politicians, the gendered assumptions about politicians are manifest in the discourses used. The differential use of language signals the media's opprobrium against women who transgress the orthodox boundaries of what proper women are and what they should (are allowed to) do. What they don't do, apparently, is become politicians. "If a woman goes out at 6 o'clock in the morning to clean offices to keep her family together, to raise her children, she will be presented as a heroine. If she wants to run that office she will be presented as an unnatural woman and even worse, as an unnatural mother" (Glenda Jackson, Labour, U.K.).

PORTRAITS OF ELITE WOMEN II:
HILLARY, SARAH, AND THE POLITICS OF SHAME

The U.S. presidential elections afforded yet another opportunity to consider the ways in which the media are fascinated by women parliamentarians. Although this is certainly not the place to undertake an in-depth analysis of the ways in which coverage of Hillary Rodham Clinton and Sarah Palin was distinctively different to that of John McCain, Joe Biden, and Barack Obama, even the most casual news consumer could not fail to have recognized that *something* was going on. From the time she made her candidacy known, Clinton was haunted by the specter of husband Bill, damned by association. Any number of articles, both straight and of the lampoon variety, quipped that with Hillary you got two for the price of one, and almost immediately she was framed as jumping on the bandwagon of Bill's popularity in a sleight of hand which obscured her formal political experience. Coverage of Palin also peddled the same line of inexperience, pointing to the tiny population of Alaska over which she had hitherto had dominion. While Obama was scarcely the seasoned politician either, news media stories did not dismiss his credentials in quite the same way, instead suggesting that his activist and campaigning background would stand him in good stead and, importantly, he was not tainted by past misdemeanors perpetrated by his partner. He was also framed as the solid family man with solid family values, unlike Palin whose seventeen year old, unmarried daughter, Bristol, hit the headlines only days after Palin was confirmed as the vice presidential nominee, because she was pregnant by her student boyfriend. While the Republican campaign team cranked into action immediately, insisting that Bristol's pregnancy was indicative of Palin's antiabortion stance, it soon became clear that the Romeo and Juliet romance was, like the play, doomed to fail.

Accusations of media sexism have long been articulated and the high visibility of two differently controversial women in the U.S. presidential campaign once again rehearsed the for/against arguments and once again pitted the media against politicians and women-focused campaign groups. For the media, journalists simply dismissed the criticism of sexism put by the Clinton camp as being a cynical strategy to find reasons for why she lost the vote. However, in an ironic twist, Katie Couric, who became infamous for her interviews with Palin in which she managed to wrong-foot the hapless politician several times, subsequently commented, "Like her or not, one of the great lessons of that [Clinton's] campaign is the continued—and accepted—role of sexism in American life, particularly in the media" (Seelye and Bosman 2008, n.p.) Similarly, Candy Crowley who covered the campaign for CNN said that while the regular news was done "straight," the commentaries showed clear evidence of sexism. In her concession speech, Clinton herself alluded to the continuation of media sexism at a time when racist reporting had almost been obliterated. While all branches of the media are implicated, most commentators suggest that cable TV stations were particularly poisonous. For example, MSNBC host Chris Matthews described Clinton as a "she-devil" and colleague Tucker Carlson said that when Clinton came on TV, he involuntarily crossed his legs (Seelye and Bosman 2008). On the activist side, the National Organization of Women launched a Media Hall of Shame website to which they uploaded examples of sexist reporting and urged Obama to start a national debate on sexism.

Even male bloggers felt compelled to comment on the obvious sexism which pervaded news coverage of the Palin and Clinton campaign trails. For example, C. J. Maloney expressed his surprise at the way in which the cameras kept panning to Sarah Palin's rear view during the actually rather important vice presidential debate between her and Joe Biden, asking, "Is that normal?" (2009).Well, such a preoccupation with women's corporeal rather than intellectual features is sadly entirely normal practice for contemporary news media. Even when there is a relatively positive report on the performance of female politicians, the discourse is often grudging, as in this report of the Palin-Biden debate from the *Guardian*: "Although she frequently betrayed nerves early in the debate, hurrying out words and ideas, she made no gaffes, other than referring to the U.S. commander in Afghanistan, David McKiernan, as General McClellan" (MacAskill 2008). Commenting on her performance herself, in an interview with Fox News the day after the debate, Palin said that she thought it had gone well, although she felt she had been "clobbered" by the news media more generally.

The Mommy Card

While both Clinton and Palin played the mommy card, the strategy worked to greater or lesser degrees for each candidate. For Clinton it was mostly successful because she could parade Chelsea at numerous functions and her daughter was savvy enough to be able to rally eloquently for her mom and the media mostly left her alone. Palin was treated rather less gently and for every report which promised Palin's appeal to working mothers was another lambasting the "mother of five" for leaving her children to fend for themselves, with special opprobrium leveled against Palin's unmotherly decision to abandon her disabled infant of four months. Her strong, right-wing views on issues such as abortion and welfare also created complicated responses to her candidacy as a woman: during her nineteen months as governor and two terms as a small-town mayor, she proposed cutting $1.5 million in child care subsidies in her first budget plan, according to news accounts (Amon 2008). This meant that her potential voting base was divided not just along party and gender lines, but also bisected by her views on such controversial issues.

> "The fact that Palin is a mother of five who has a 4-month-old child, a woman who is juggling work and family responsibilities, will speak to many women," said Kim Gandy, chairwoman of the National Organization for Women PAC. "But will Palin speak for women? Based on her record and her stated positions, the answer is clearly no." (Gandy quoted in Amon 2008, n.p.)

> "She is the total feminist," said Florence Scarinci of Franklin Square, a registered Democrat and the Long Island liaison for the antiabortion group Feminists Choosing Life. "She is an intelligent, achieving woman who doesn't believe you have to choose between your career, your education and your family." (Scarinci quoted in Amon 2008, n.p.)

Still others simply saw McCain's decision to stablemate Palin as pure cynicism, shoring up a diminishing voter base by embodying, literally, the characteristics which McCain palpably lacked as well as replaying the invidious game of least worst: a white woman OR an African American man, some choice. Howze (2008, n.p.) is clear that Palin really did tick all the right boxes: young, female, mother, outsider, hunts and shoots, against abortion, biracial husband, suggesting somewhat cynically that she was "less a running mate, more a collection of polling qualities."

Poacher Turned Gatekeeper

In an effort to deflect criticism, the news media have been quick to identify the ways in which political parties themselves were not averse to bad-mouthing their own side as well as the competition. One of the primary targets of academic criticism of media bias against women politicians, Fox News, ran a number of stories during the U.S. primaries which featured negative comments made about Hillary Clinton by both John Edwards and Barack Obama. "Sen. Barack Obama and John Edwards sharpened their attacks on Democratic presidential frontrunner Sen. Hillary Clinton Tuesday, taking swipes at her character and use of 'textbook' political strategies that they say prove she'll say anything to get elected" (Fox News 2007a, n.p.). However, as Democrat consultant Stephanie Cutter argues, while attack advertising is commonplace between competing parties, it can sometimes backfire when directed at one's own colleagues, especially someone as high profile as Hillary Clinton (Cutter cited in Fox News 2007a). The Clinton camp retaliated by putting a number of the Edwards/Obama criticisms on her campaign website as examples of unfair campaign practice. Fox News even went as far as including findings from an October 2007 survey which showed that Clinton received the most negative media coverage of any of the White House field (Fox News 2007b), clearly implying that it was nothing to do with them. "Senator Edwards' entire campaign has devolved into a daily routine of negative personal attacks against Senator Clinton," said Clinton spokesman Phil Singer. "He's a far cry from the John Edwards of 2004 who rose to prominence by decrying personal attacks against other Democrats" (Fox News 2007b).

The Same Old, Same Old

In 2009, even though Hillary Clinton and Sarah Palin *could* have achieved the top job in the White House, their sex remains the most newsworthy thing about them. One of Spain's most popular newspapers,

20 Minutos, ran a survey on the world's most beautiful women politicians showing Palin at number 24 and Clinton at number 34 in a list that featured fifty-plus female politicians from thirty countries, including Japan, Russia, and Italy (Jones 2009). The newspaper makes the point that Clinton, at age sixty-one, was the oldest on the list with the youngest named as Julia Bonk [*sic*] from Germany, at twenty-two years old. No British women featured in the list and a spokesperson from the newspapers suggested that British women MPs are not famed for their beauty, but added, somewhat incredulously, that "when you look at women politicians worldwide some of them really are very attractive." It is very easy to get too po-faced about media coverage, and after all, individuals choose to run for elected office, but the extent of media sexism is sometimes so extreme that it is hard to believe that it is *not* harmful to women's interests.

The sexist and even misogynistic frames used by news media have a long pedigree, labeling them as monsters or nonwomen, characterizing women's voices as hard to listen to/impossible to take seriously, criticizing women for the misdemeanors of their partners. While the tabloids are often seen as the primary culprits, mainstream media are not averse to such strategies, so that the *New York Times* wrote of Hillary Clinton's "cackle" and the *Washington Post* spoke of her cleavage. However, the levels of venality and ridicule are sometimes breathtaking. McEwan (2009, n.p.) considers the discussion of the signing of the Economic Recovery Bill in February 2009 on a radio show hosted by right-winger, Peter Boyles. The bill-signing ceremony in Denver was attended by Democratic Representative Diana DeGette. "Boyles repeatedly referred to DeGette (pronounced with a hard *G*) as 'Vagina DeGette' or 'Vagina DeJet.' Sure, she may be a member of the United States Congress, but, more importantly, she's a woman—and women aren't anything more than their vaginas, anyway." To those who continue to ask, what's the problem, this quote makes clear what the answer is. Although Hillary Clinton and Sarah Palin did not make history by becoming the first female U.S. president or the first female U.S. vice president respectively, Palin did achieve a first in that she is the first vice presidential nominee to have a porn movie made specifically with her in mind, titled *Nailin' Paylin* (Maloney 2009).

THE SO-WHAT QUESTION—
DID THE MEDIA DO FOR SOCCER MOM?

Immediately after the vice presidential debate between Palin and Biden, two separate polls suggested that Palin's "folksy" appeal failed to hit the mark. A CBS News poll reported that 46 percent of voters who described themselves as "uncommitted" thought Biden had won compared with 21 percent of respondents who felt that Palin had performed better. A CNN poll found that voters were divided 51 to 39 percent, Biden to Palin. However, when politicians themselves were polled, some—Democrats as well as Republicans—gave Palin a draw and even a narrow win (MacAskill 2008). However, in the end, Palin did not manage to change McCain's fortunes, possibly because her nomination was seen as simply a cynical Republican ploy to rehabilitate McCain as a bit more in touch with the younger generation and/or appeal to women voters. Importantly, the result demonstrated the limitations of the critical mass thesis for improving the lot of women, since it's not just about more women, it's about more of the right kind of women. Women voters will not vote for a candidate just because of their shared sex and Obama's campaign was a very well-executed one, designed to appeal to precisely those hard-to-reach audiences of young people and members of ethnic minorities, half of whom are women. Even disgruntled Hillary supporters were never likely to vote for Sarah just because they wanted to see a woman in the White House, albeit as vice president, especially a woman who espoused such hard-line views on sensitive issues such as abortion.

Palin did not receive unremittingly harsh media coverage because her accident-prone early performances under the media spotlight highlighted her inexperience and nerves and subsequently led to her routine depiction as a stupid and dangerous, gun-toting girl from Hicksville whose finger was rather too ready to push the red button. Allied to these fears were the abundant stories about her liking for expensive clothes, her religious fundamentalism, and her propensity to use taxpayer money to fund holidays for her family, not to mention the usual sexist questioning about whether a mother of five was capable or competent to hold high political office (Wildman 2008). Recently, Palin gave an interview to radio talk show host John Zeigler who is making a documentary in which he intends to "evidence" that media malpractice was at the root of Obama's eventual victory. In that conversation, Palin suggests that relations between her and the news handlers on the McCain campaign team were tense almost from the beginning of her nomination and implies that she was set up to fail by her own side.

In the wake of the 2008 presidential elections, media pundits speculate that Palin is now squaring up to run for president in 2012. In early 2009, she launched a new campaigning entity, SarahPAC, which will enable her to fund-raise and in the summer of the same year, she resigned from her governorship. But while Palin herself bemoans, mostly rightly, her harsh media coverage—it's possible to hate her politics but sympathize with her media experiences—some commentators argue that in the end all publicity is good publicity for a politician, not least because brand recognition is both important and a way to maintain visibility in an otherwise crowded media landscape (Pilkington 2009a). If Palin really does believe that the treatment of herself and her family by the media is a consequence of a conspiracy perpetrated by the elite liberal corps of journalists—a class-based rather than sex-based analysis—then it's a conspiracy which is doing her no harm at all at the moment, as eyes continue to follow her tracks at a time when other presidential contenders such as Hillary Clinton have all but disappeared from view.

GENDER, MEDIA, AND EFFECT

If the public is to be able to discriminate between different candidates and their policies and thus make an informed choice about who they want to lead and govern them, then they must "acquire sufficient information about matters under public discussion to avoid being easily duped about the facts by self-interested candidate misinformation or distortion" (Buchanan 1991, 22). What Buchanan is implying here, although not quite saying, is that the political default position is one where the category "politician" (i.e., that they're all pretty much the same) is more rather than less likely to manipulate the voter/public, so the latter needs to be awake to evidence of willful intent to deceive. The agenda-setting power of the mass media has been well-documented over the past few decades (Iyengar 1987; Ansolabehere, Behr, and Iyengar 1991; Entman 2007) to a point where it is now believed that the media's impact is less about actively changing values and beliefs than about determining what issues are important. The extent to which media scholars cede power to media organizations has also shifted considerably. Successive studies of the media's portrayal of women politicians and political candidates are unequivocal in their findings that the sex of politicians is an important factor in the differential coverage that women and men politicians receive at the hands of the media and that this differentiated coverage may have important effects on how candidates are evaluated by the electorate (Ross 2002; Bystrom et al. 2004; Aalberg and Jenssen 2007). Caroline Flint, one of the so-called Blair's Babes who was elected along with 101 other Labour women MPs in the 1997 British elections, is exasperated with a media discourse which is only interested in her views on facilities in the House of Commons.

> [I am] ready to throttle the next journalist who asks me about toilets and crèches in the House of Commons. . . . There are enough toilets for women MPs . . . and as for the crèche—there are very few women with children under five. They [the media] should focus on the diversity of women in Parliament. We are a mixed bunch and hopefully in many different ways represent the variety of women in Britain. (Flint cited in McDougall 1998, 79)

The ways in which women candidates and parliamentarians are covered by news media find obvious parallels with the way in which women and women's issues more generally are marginalized within media discourse: while a particularly gendered item might make the women's page in daily newspapers, it will rarely feature as a news item in the mainstream sections (Kahn and Goldenberg 1997). The media's persistent domestication of women parliamentarians and the power of media workers to frame their female subjects as constantly in thrall to their bodily functions send out clear messages to the public that this is indeed what preoccupies our women politicians. In Kahn's (1994) comparative study of American Senate candidates during the 1982 and 1986 elections, she found that women generally received less media attention than men and that this could adversely affect their chances because less information about candidates could mean that intending voters knew little about the specific policy positions of women candidates and there-fore voter recognition of women candidates was weak. Kahn also found that the substance of media coverage was qualitatively different; for example, more time was devoted to the horse race element of women's campaigns than their policy positions.

WHO SPEAKS IS WHO COUNTS

When challenged, journalists will often say that they don't cover stories focused on women politicians because there are relatively few women in positions of authority, either in government or in opposition parties. Although this is becoming less true, it is nonetheless seen as a legitimate excuse for marginalizing women's voices. However, what is less excus-able are the ways in which journalists, either through laziness or tight deadlines or any other of the reasons they put forward, tend to use the same (nonpolitical) sources as expert commentators. Given what has be-come conventional wisdom about sourcing more generally, that is, that journalists will tend to use people like themselves who share the same opinions and will not elect to use quotes with which they disagree in their own reports (Manning 2001), decisions about which sources to use become a little more explicable. As most journalists are men and most politicians, business leaders, and senior executives are also men, then a male-ordered circuit of the same old, same old is repeated endlessly in this buddy-buddy world. The journalistic predilection for using mostly "official" sources means that the kinds of news we receive are the sani-tized and official versions. How journalists gather news, who they use as sources, and which quotes from those sources they actually incorporate into their stories all combine to produce a constructed *version* of reality, both of the particular story or event in question, but more broadly, of the *type* of society.

Feminist media research which has focused specifically on the use of women and men as sources for news reports provides predictable and disheartening conclusions (Leibler and Smith 1997; Zoch and VanSlyke Turk 1998; Ross 2007). In a large-scale study of women and television in Europe in the mid-1980s (twenty-five channels in ten countries), 1,236 news stories were analyzed over a composite week: of the individuals interviewed in all those items, a mere 16 percent were women (Gallagher 1988). In Zoch and VanSlyke Turk's study, the researchers set out to explore, among other things, the gender variable in sourcing, analyzing a sample of stories over the decade 1986–1996 in a number of U.S. newspapers. Of the 1,126 stories which were coded, the researchers found that only 20 percent of named sources were women. "Since length is one cue journalists give to importance in a story (longer is more important), it appears, then, that male stories were quoted more frequently in the longer, more important stories, and were more trusted than women to give the longer, more in-depth quote" (Zoch and VanSlyke Turk 1998, 769–770).

If there are relatively few women nuclear scientists and a current news debate is around nuclear testing, sourcing men as experts has a logic, but what about when the views of the ordinary woman and man on the street are being canvased? Surely there is absolutely no reason why similar numbers of women and men should not be asked to comment on an issue of the day, especially at times when opinion poll results are constantly quoted in the media, such as during general elections? In studies which focus specifically on the incorporation of the public into news and political discourse, those which look at the gender dimension of who is asked to speak show that men are much more likely to be invited than women (Hernandez 1995; Stephenson 1998; Wykes 1998; WACC 2000; Ross 2007). When a woman *is* invited to speak, it is mostly in her role as mother, her biology defining her authority to give voice. In a study of the British radio phone-in show *Election Call*, broadcast during the 2001 general election, around one-third of the callers who were selected were women (Ross 2004) and a much larger study of British citizens and public access programming showed an even lower percentage of women contributing to such shows (McNair, Hibberd, and Schlesinger 2003). However, it should be said that overall the view of *any* ordinary person is not routinely sought in news reports because of the privileging of elite voices over Joanne and Joe Public (Lewis, Inthorn, and Wahl-Jorgensen 2005).

Any number of studies suggest that the composition of newsroom staff in terms of the balance of women and men influences the content produced by that newsroom, if not always a different focus, then certainly a different tone and style, because women have different experiences in the world and thus bring a different perspective (Steiner 1998; de Bruin 2000; Melin-Higgins 2004). In Rodgers and Thorson's study (2003), they found that female and male journalists practiced a differentiated journalism in terms of style, tone, and sources used, but that these differences were most marked in smaller newsrooms and where there was a more even balance between women and men newsworkers. This suggests that larger newsrooms with a predominance of male staff strongly encourage a conformist outlook which produces hegemonic journalistic output in terms of "routinizing" a male-ordered perspective, a finding echoed by other studies of gendered journalism (see also Van Zoonen 1998; Robinson 2005).

One of the ways in which women journalists "do" journalism which is identifiably different to their male colleagues is precisely in their use of sources. In most studies, men dominate as sources and Shoemaker and Reese (1996) found that men were twice as likely as women to be featured as subjects or sources in newspaper articles (see also DeLano Brown et al. 1987; Liebler and Smith 1997). Similarly, Zoch and VanSlyke Turk (1998) looked at the topic focus of stories in relation to source selection in three U.S. newspapers over a ten-year period (1986–1996) and suggest that women rarely feature in news of national or international importance. Armstrong's analysis of gender as an influencing factor in the use of female and male sources found that male sources were much more prevalent than female ones (Armstrong 2004). Interestingly and optimistically, both Zoch and VanSlyke Turk and Armstrong found that women journalists are far more likely to use women as sources in their items than their male colleagues. However, in my own work on this topic (Ross 2007), I found no such positive correlation, so different national contexts can produce vastly different results, not least because of differences in professional cultures.

WOMEN AND NEWSWORK

However, if we assume that there is *some* kind of relationship between who *produces* news and the *content* of news reports, then mapping the involvement of women in news industries is an important aspect of understanding the gender-news relationship. During the 1990s, a number of studies across the world attempted to map women's employ-ment within media organizations. The trend revealed by such statistical analyses shows that in Western media generally, women experience the glass ceiling effect, where they seem to make steady progress as new en-trants into the sector but then do not go on to achieve senior positions. In Finland, for example, the number of women in media industries far outstrips that of men (Zilliacus-Tikkanen 1997) but their progression to decision-making positions continues to be minimal. In Lünenborg's (1996) study of nine European countries, women accounted for more than one-quarter of all reporter, subeditor, and editor posts but occu-pied a mere 12 percent of editorial executive positions. In the United States and Canada the volume indicators are broadly the same with a similarly poor showing of women at the top (see Norris 1997; Carter, Branston, and Allan 1998; Robinson 2005).

When considering the status which women *do* achieve, it is clear that their involvement in the decision-making tier of media organizations has been extremely modest thus far. At the turn of the twenty-first century in the United States, women comprised only 24 percent of television news directors and 20 percent of radio news directors, according to the 2001 Women and Minorities Survey conducted by the U.S.-based Radio and Television News Directors Association and Foundation. Similarly, a study published by the Annenberg Public Policy Center (2002) found that across telecommunications and electronic commerce (e-commerce) industries women make up only 13 percent of top executives and only 9 percent of individuals on boards of directors. Women comprise slightly more than a quarter of local TV news directors, 17 percent of local TV general managers, and only 13 percent of general managers at radio stations. Byerly's (2001) analysis of the six major media corporations revealed only seven women at board level and a further seven women occupying chief executive officer positions. In her review of research on women in media decision making from the 1970s to the 1990s, Rush (2001) argues that the ratio of women to men in journalism and mass communication fields has remained more or less stable, moving from 1:4 to 1:3 over the past three decades. And so on and so on.

The incorporation of women journalists into a traditionally male pro-fession such as journalism has had the effect of normalizing what are essentially male-identified concerns and a male-directed agenda. Thus, acceptance of a journalistic practice and set of conventions based on unchallenged and apparently unproblematic news routines allows male perspectives to be constructed as neutral and uncontroversial and, most importantly, to appear as value-free (Komter 1991). In work undertaken with women working on metropolitan newspapers in South Africa, Gillwald found that "few journalists, even those dissatisfied with discriminatory allocation of news stories, were aware of the 'male-centricity' of what they saw as standard journalistic practice—newsworthiness, readability, public interest" (1994, 27). Some women in Gillwald's study were not only apparently gender blind but used the convenient example of their own success as a means by which to refute the suggestion of sexism in the industry. This strategy of self-deception or, at best, a refusal to empathize with the real experiences of other women was mirrored in the responses of some of the women who took part in my own study of women journalists, responses which neatly exemplified an internalized sexism which places the blame for women's lack of professional progress squarely back in their own hands (Ross 2001).

Newsroom culture which masquerades as a neutral and professional journalism ethos is, for all practical (and ideological) purposes, actually organized around a man-as-norm and woman-as-interloper structure and these structures are remarkably similar and remarkably stable over temporal and geographical dimensions, as ample empirical and anecdotal evidence shows. For example, the experiences of women journalists in Aida Opoku-Mensah's (2004) study of African newsrooms was broadly comparable to those discussed in Ammu Joseph's (2004) study of Indian newsrooms. Women who choose to work in these male-ordered domains must develop strategies which usually involve either beating the boys at their own game or else developing alternative ways of practicing journalism. This latter is often achieved by working in concert with other professionals who are also on the outside of the inner circle by dint of the same or different reasons for exclusion, for example, journalists of color, self-identified gay and lesbian journalists, and so on (see also Byerly 2004).[7] How women deal with the typical newsroom culture will of course depend on any number of personal, professional, and experiential factors and such strategies can include (following Melin-Higgins and Djerf-Pierre 1998) *incorporation* (one of the boys), which requires women to take on so-called masculine styles, values, and reporting behaviors such as "objectivity"; *feminist*, where journalists make a conscious decision to provide an alternative voice, for example, writing on health in order to expose child abuse and rape; and *retreat*, where women choose to work as freelancers rather than continue to fight battles in the workplace. Interestingly, although Melin-Higgins and Djerf-Pierre regard women's exit from mainstream media as a "retreat," many women media workers see their decision to quit as assertive and empowering. For these women, stepping into the light of alternative media production is an exciting and liberating escape, even though the uncertain future of such work provokes a range of different anxieties.

HARASSMENT IN THE NEWSROOM

The few studies which have focused specifically on sexist and discriminatory behavior have found overwhelming evidence of both subtle and overt harassment against women staff. Research by Weaver (1992) in the United States revealed that between 40 and 60 percent of female journalists who took part in his study had had direct experience of harassment. More than half the women and just over a quarter of men who took part in Sieghart and Henry's (1998) study of British journalists said that they had either experienced and/or witnessed discrimination against women, with newspaper environments being more likely to produce discriminatory behaviors than magazines. In yet another study, 60 out of 227 participating journalists believe that sexual harassment is a problem for women in the industry with 10 percent also stating that they had personal experience of harassment (Walsh-Childer, Chance, and Herzog 1996). The kinds of harassment described in that study varied from degrading comments to sexual assault and approximately 17 percent of the study's participants reported having experienced physical sexual harassment at least "sometimes." Byerly and Warren's (1996) study cites the experience of one woman reporter who was considered to have an aggressive reporting style, and who was given a jock strap as a farewell present by her male colleagues with the words "sniff this for luck" written on the band. More subtle but equally pernicious examples of harassment are not hard to find. In interviews carried out with women journalists in South Africa by Byerly and Ross (2006), we found clear anxieties about how women's internal promotion would be viewed by their colleagues, precisely because a woman's advancement was routinely characterized as the fruits of her sexual labors.

> You find that if a woman gets a job they will say, something else was going on. They don't even look at your work, the first thing that comes to their mind is no, there has to be something else like you've been sleeping with somebody, you're involved in one way or another with somebody and sometimes you really feel, well, OK, I'll do this [go for promotion] but what is going to be the perception of other people? Will they think that I got this because of my own work or will they start talking around and saying all the nasty things that they can say. (Thandazo)[8]

Similarly, in North's work (2007) with Australian journalists, she found that a number of different forms of sexual harassment were reported by her women interviewees, although few named it as such and none were prepared to pursue a complaint for fear of being ostracized. Notwithstanding the notion that, following Butler (1997), gender is about performance rather than biology, women and men occupy different subject positions in professional occupations, including in the newsroom, and women can choose to respond to sexual harassment in at least three ways: acceptance, denial, challenge. Which choice is made will depend on any number of different factors which are associated with both the woman in question as an individual, including her determination to campaign versus her desire to fit in, as well as the specifics of the environment in which she works, including her support networks, the existence of empathetic colleagues, line managers, and so on. North (2007, 92) makes clear that both women and men are affected by a newsroom environment which tolerates or even encourages sexual harassment.

> Sexually harassing behaviour as a (repeated) practice creates gendered journalists, in its male initiated challenge/assault, in how it makes women feel, in how they respond, and in how they are understood by others. . . . When female journalists enter the industry sexually harassing behaviour is just one of the many ways in which they are excluded, marginalised, and in some cases become outsiders. But women do survive and indeed succeed even in the face of it. When male journalists enter the industry, engag-

ing in sexually harassing behaviour of women is one of the many ways in which some occupy the privileged position of an insider.

But women newsworkers have fought back against unfair practices in the newsroom, especially in the United States, where a number of high profile court cases have served to keep the disgrace of gender discrimination in the public arena. One of the best known cases involved Christine Craft who fought a long-drawn-out campaign against her employer, the Kansas City television station KMBC.[9] In the end, Craft lost her suit, but her successor at the station, Brenda Williams, also filed a discrimination case against the station and settled for $100,000. One of the largest suits was won by Janet Peckinpaugh ($8.3 million) against WFSB-TV in Hartford, Connecticut, but as Chambers, Steiner, and Fleming (2004) point out, such wins have served as scant deterrent for stations who continue to fire women staff once they reach their thirties. In the United Kingdom, the "resignation" of African Caribbean newsreader Moira Stewart from the BBC prompted considerable speculation about whether she was just the latest casualty of the BBC's efforts to replace professional maturity with beautiful youth (the two are inevitably mutually exclusive in the BBC's eyes.

WRITING IT DOWN

However, there is a creditable history of women's efforts to change the picture, both for themselves and for other women, and Chambers, Steiner, and Fleming discuss the development of such efforts, from the first wave of suffrage publications in the early part of the twentieth century to feminism's second and third waves, which mapped onto the political waves of feminism throughout the past century. As the authors point out, although this early history has been almost entirely neglected by historians, "reform and activist groups invested heavily in periodicals to disseminate their ideas, especially when access to existing mainstream publications was blocked" (168).

During the 1970s and 1980s, there were hundreds of feminist publications published in the United Kingdom and the United States, albeit many were very short-lived and addressed a highly specialized audience.

For example, one directory listing lesbian and gay periodicals published over most of the twentieth century cited 2,678 publications (Miller 1990). One immediate impact of the 1969 Stonewall riots in New York City, an event ushering in the gay liberation movement, was the blossoming of a number of local and regional publications aimed at lesbian and gay audiences with titles such as *Amazon, Dyke,* and *Lesbian Feminists*. One magazine which enjoyed a relatively long shelf life for an alternative publication was the British *Spare Rib*, set up in 1972 and enjoying twenty-one years of often controversial but never dull publication until its final liquidation in 1993. As with many magazines produced by collectives, *Spare Rib* was often beset by internal struggles over ideology and meaning and what was legitimate content for a feminist magazine. A newer magazine which exploits the significant developments in e-zine publishing is *Bitch!*, founded in 1996.

> On the impulse to give a voice to the vast numbers of us who know in our hearts that these [stereotypical] images [of women] are false, and want something to replace them. We want to see images of women as smart and capable as we know we are. We want to find those women out there who are articulating with things like writing, film, art, music, and feminist t-shirt businesses, the experiences that Hollywood and Madison Avenue refuse to admit exist. (*Bitch*, premiere issue 1, vol. 1, Winter)[10]

AND FINALLY . . .

What an analysis of women's representation in news demonstrates, incontrovertibly, is that the media's framing (in every sense of the word) of women in highly restricted and mostly negative ways is not simply the consequence of the idiosyncrasies of this newspaper or that TV channel or that radio station but rather is a *global* phenomenon which has endured over time and across media formats, and continues to do so. The fruits of all the various research studies briefly discussed above have interesting but ultimately depressing things to say about how news media portray women's role and function in modern societies, not least that the most common way for women to feature as subjects in news stories is as victim, especially of sexual violence. The news media are primary contributors to public debate on violence and play a crucial cultural function in their use of explicitly gendered frames in news reportage. As Allan points out, "reports of male violence being perpetrated against women have appeared in the news on a routine basis since the emergence of popular newspapers in the nineteenth century" (Allan 1999, 149). And the ways in which the media continue to contribute to this circulation of passive and victimized femininity is through the repetitive framing of woman as victim, woman as object, woman as body. These frames are routinized and normalized, endlessly recycled to protect a male-ordered status quo. Women remain always less than the sum of their body parts. The blatant sexism of some of the tabloid press, for example, the British tabloid *Sunday Sport*'s regular pullout of almost-nude women with its attendant slogan—"Ave it!"— provides an apposite comment on the place of women in the news: we are there to be *had*.

Even taking the most generous view of the media's role in the articulation of a normative social world order which privileges men and male concerns over those of women—that is, as unwitting agent of control—it is nonetheless irresistible to contend that there must be *some* element of complicity, some sense of collusion with the circulation of words and pictures which routinize what it is to be female and male in contemporary society. And it is precisely the "packaging" of women (following Franklin 1997) which we need to read more carefully. If news is a commodity and we are all consumers, then how women are "sold" to us in qualitative and quantitative terms is as important as how often they appear in the news: volume matters but context matters more.

But . . . some women *are* making a difference and it would be wrong not to signal that we *have* moved forward, often as a result of the efforts of courageous women newsworkers. Change happens alongside recalcitrance as activists address media bias, discrimination, and exclusion in systematic ways and push the agenda forward. For example, as a consequence of the publication of the Gender and Media Baseline Study in 2003, the South African News Editors Forum (SANEF) agreed at their annual general meeting (AGM) that same year that they would make renewed efforts to improve the representation of women in their media, and thus far, workshops and discussions have taken place in several key newsrooms across South Africa.[11] Such initiatives give us cause for hope and provide a welcome respite from the otherwise rather depressing mediascape which privileges stories of women's violation over stories of women's achievement, and especially crimes against women where the victim is apparently "just asking for it."

> WOMEN TOLD "DRINK LESS" TO AVOID RAPE. A police chief sparks controversy today by suggesting the number of rapes in Scotland could be substantially reduced if women drank less. Neil Richardson, assistant chief constable of Lothian and Borders Police, bases his claim on new research which identified victims' alcohol consumption as significant in a third of attacks. The senior officer said "a lot" of the 1,100 rapes a year could be prevented "by people not allowing themselves to be in a vulnerable position." (Richardson cited in Foster, *Scotland on Sunday*, June 11, 2006, n.p.)

> When a sex victim is labeled as attractive, she usually receives less sympathy. This is so ingrained [in news discourse] that even when sympathies are overwhelmingly with the victim, descriptions of her physical appearance invoke the myth that she provoked it. (Boyle 2006, 76)

While women's involvement in the news industry as media professionals has had some impact on improving the ways in which women are presented and how women experience newsroom culture, these gains have been modest and haphazard. Increasing the numbers of women working in the industry is insufficient to promote lasting change because what is required is a significant culture shift in the industry as a whole, where the benefits of such shifts must be quantifiable. One such benefit is the increased readership and viewership of women to news media, if the content can finally be made to match their interests: the feminization of news media can be seen as an explicit response to make news more acceptable to women consumers (see also Brewer 2007; Poindexter, Meraz, and Schmitz 2008). To quote Clinton's campaign advisor, "It's the economy, stupid," and without attention to the bottom line, lasting and meaningful change in news or any other industry will be hard to achieve.

FURTHER READING

Allan, S. ed. (2005). *Journalism: Critical Issues*. Maidenhead, U.K.: Open University Press.

Boyle, K. (2006). *Media and Violence*. London: Sage.

Byerly, C. M., and Ross, K. (2006). *Women and Media: A Critical Introduction*. Malden, Mass.: Blackwell Publishing.

Bystrom, D. G., Banwart, M. C., Kaid, L. L., and Robertson, T. A. (2004). *Gender and Candidate Communication*. New York: Routledge.

Meehan, E. R., and Riordan, E. (2002). *Sex and Money: Feminism and Political Economy in the Media*. Minneapolis and London: University of Minnesota Press.

Robinson, G. (2005). *Gender, Journalism and Equity: Canadian, U.S. and European Perspectives*. Cresskill, N.J.: Hampton.

5

GENDER@INTERNET

Within the various paradigms of technology and capitalist development, it is important to consider gender in addition to technologies
and context as a way to understand both the paradoxes and contradictions that perpetuate inequities, while at the same time celebrat-
ing the possibilities that these technologies allow. (Cooks and Isgro
2003, 351)

The exponential and ferociously evolving technology which is the Internet has been a preoccupying interest for many media researchers for
the past few years, with commentators euphorically optimistic about the
technology's potential or mordantly disturbed by its perversions, in almost equal measure. While theories, grand and otherwise, abound (see
Rheingold 1993; Negroponte 1995; Castells 1996; Virilio 1997; Plant
1997), and this is not the place to discuss that already vast literature, I
want to focus in this chapter on those aspects of the Internet which are
specifically concerned with gender and gender difference. In particular,
we will consider those differences in terms of what women and men
do differently when they go online, the gendered aspects of the digital
divide, how women and men talk to each other and between themselves, women's networking, and the development of women friendly
websites.

How women and men (differently) experience this medium is incredibly important for its future development, especially in terms of how we, as both consumers and increasingly producers of Net-based content, might exert influence over its future direction. Historically, women have found it difficult to come to voice in media contexts, let alone exercise any power over shaping the contours of the media landscape, but does the general lack of gatekeeping across the virtual sky enhance our ability to nudge the medium in ways which are simply unthinkable in terms of traditional media? Ways, moreover, which begin to subvert the gendered power relations which characterize pretty much every other aspect of our social, cultural, and economic lives, moving us toward a more inclusive environment where our voices, in all their glorious timbres, can be heard. Some of these issues are discussed below. I don't promise to provide too many answers but rather rehearse some of the debates around the possibilities and practices of a gendered (cyber)space.

IT'S A MAN'S WORLD, ISN'T IT?

Some feminist thinkers consider that science, in its multiple manifestations including the Internet, is irrevocably located within a male-dominated sphere and functions (and has evolved) in direct response to men's needs and men's interests, serving patriarchy in spectacular style. Partly, this view is informed by the historical antecedents of the Internet which are rooted in war and developed as part of a military strategy to link computers together to improve intrasite communications in a cold war environment, known as ARPANET (Wasserman and Richmond-Abbott 2005). Such a command-and-control provenance makes perceiving the technology as male quite straightforward: men make war, men make the Internet, men use the Internet, thus the Internet is *for* men. However, while this may have been true in the early days of the Internet's development, and a gendered digital divide (as well as other discriminations such as class, ethnicity, and geography) is still evident in the new millennium as discussed below, things are a bit more complicated now, genderwise. So, our Net-based discussions must include but also move beyond the simple framing of women as hapless victims of patriarchy's whimsical proclivities toward a consideration of what we do with and to

the technology and not simply what it does to and with *us*. This impulse
to see beyond the comfortable binaries of gender conflict reflects the
kinds of shifts we have observed when researching other media forms
when agency is better understood (see Hall 1973), even as we also acknowledge the barriers which still exist in realizing its full potential.

BEING AND DOING ONLINE: THE GENDER AGENDA

All research with human subjects is necessarily fixed in time, even studies about virtual space. Interviews are conducted, e-mails sent, online
questionnaires completed and analyzed, findings written. This is the
way of research: it captures and freezes a moment in time, at the time of
my research, *this* is what I found. However, with a medium such as the
Internet, which is, even after twenty years of more or less mainstream
existence, still emergent, still relatively unknown, all our findings can
only *ever* be contingent. Of course this is more or less the case with *all*
research else we would never move forward to challenge allegedly immutable orthodoxies. Shifts in our developing understanding of social
phenomena forces shifts in mores and mind-sets, such that replicating
a study five years after the first time might produce very different results. But with the Internet this problem of temporality is more acute
because the technology really is moving at an incredible pace. Identified
problems with connectivity in Mombassa one year might be resolved a
few weeks later by better cabling: the poor uptake of Internet services
in an Athens primary school might be summarily fixed by a government policy to put a computer in every classroom. The noisy arrival of
YouTube and MySpace onto the web scene, and their almost instant
replacement by the next generation of social networking sites such as
Facebook and Bebo could not have been foreseen even the year before
their spectacular births. Making this point about time/space is important
when considering a medium which has still so much potential to fulfill,
still so many more places yet to explore: to paraphrase Captain Kirk,
(cyber)space really *is* the final frontier and more and more meters of it
are being conquered every day. But the crucial question is, by whom?
Reporting on the pilot phase of a longer-term project on women and
the Internet, Scott, Semmens, and Willoughby (1999) describe their

work as a story with "a fixed beginning, a contested centre and an open ending," perfectly capturing the fluidity of web-based research and the fallacy of being able to legitimately conclude *anything* which has a lasting meaning and applicability. However, of rather less ambiguity are the broad themes around women and men's use of and access to the Internet which countless studies report over and over, across a multitude of different national contexts, across at least a decade of concentrated research endeavor by feminist researchers in particular. So, notwithstanding my opening comments above, we *can* say a little about trends and themes, no matter how fleeting they are in the bigger picture of human and technological development.

Research from the early 1990s reported more men than women using the Internet, although women were more likely than men to be using computers, but for clerical and administrative tasks (Kaplan 1994) and tended to be less confident about using the Internet than men. However, a decade later, the picture was (and is) very different, with the gender gap in Internet use gradually diminishing to the point of almost parity (Bimber 2000; Norris 2001; Ono and Zavodny 2003), at least in the comfortable and Internet-friendly West. Many contemporary studies suggest that women now outnumber men among new Internet users, although this is largely because they are simply playing catch-up (Cummings and Kraut 2002). Overall, the under-twenty age group is widely acknowledged to be the definitive online user community who spend more time in cyberspace than any other age cohort. Young people thus hold the key to the Internet's enduring future success and their use of sites such as YouTube, MySpace, and Facebook make them an immensely attractive consumer group for advertisers. The acquisition of the former two sites by Rupert Murdoch and Google respectively demonstrates the potency of the teenage market in delivering revenue via online marketing strategies. Even as early as 2001, 75 percent of U.S. teenagers (twelve to seventeen years old) were reportedly online (Lenhart, Rainie, and Lewis 2001), engaged in any number of activities including instant messaging (IM), interactive games, e-mailing, seeking information, downloading music, developing web pages, and shopping. While an interest in digital technology has mostly been seen as a typically male (nerdy) preoccupation, akin to trainspotting or playing air guitar, the diversity of sites and ease of use has seen increasing numbers of girls and women getting online but what they do when they get there is often gender specific.

GENDER TRENDS

One clear trend to emerge from the literature is that women are more prevalent e-mailers than men (Howard, Rainie, and Jones 2001; Jackson et al. 2001) and men are more likely to use chat rooms than women (Wasserman and Richmond-Abbott 2005). One reason could be that chat rooms are mostly open forums and often allow quite confrontational exchanges, personalized attacks, and crude language, all of which are rarely condemned by participants. Such an environment is much less attractive to women and thus women may be less interested in getting involved in such macho discursive activities, including because they are less confident about holding their own. However, some research has suggested trends in the opposite direction, and Shaw and Gant (2002) challenge such gender-based assumptions in their experimental work which asked women and men to engage in the same Internet activity—involvement in a chat room environment—to monitor any sex-based differences in the level and character of their interactions. Their hypothesis was that users would show increased levels of support and esteem as they became more confident in the chat room and that women would show higher levels of positive valuation than men because interpersonal communication is seen as a primary activity for women online. They found that although there were increases in positive valuation among participants, gender differences were insignificant. They suggest this could be because the Generation Xers who were the subjects for the study have grown up with the Internet and therefore display similar levels of comfort and ease. Such a finding is not to disregard the vast majority of the literature which says the opposite but rather suggests that the rapid evolution of the technology and our increasing familiarization with it means that studies are out of date almost before they are published (Morahan-Martin 1998).

Most research also shows that women access relatively few sites, spend less time on the Internet, and are more likely to use the Internet from home than men (Odell 2000; Ono and Zavodny 2003). Wasserman and

Richmond-Abbott (2005) suggest that one of the reasons for this is men's more sophisticated knowledge of and confidence in using the Internet. However, as frequency of use and diversity of sites is positively correlated with confidence and knowledge, then as women become more confident, they are likely to increase the frequency and range of their Internet activities.

Another trend is that women tend to use the Internet for information retrieval and personal communication, whereas men tend to use it for entertainment by, for example, playing interactive games or downloading music (Durham 2001; Tufte 2003). For adult men, a frequent online pastime is cruising porn sites. Women are more likely to use the Internet instrumentally rather than recreationally, seeing the computer and the Internet as tools rather than technologies, and as such, say that they do not feel they need to *master* anything or exert control over cyberspace (Singh 2001).

However, one of the dangers about reading too much into research findings, especially when the focus is an endlessly forward-moving medium such as the Internet, is that trends are often transitory and research findings constantly challenge what has gone before, even just the year before, because both the technology and our use of it are constantly in flux, constantly evolving. While studies published in the late 1990s and early 2000s show particular gender trends, they soon become mere footsteps along a journey of exploration of a medium which is more or less endless. While many boys and men are playing with their virtual train sets and many girls and women are chatting on the virtual phone, many more are doing different things, even gender-bending activities. Game playing is a good example of how behaviors are changing, since current work suggests, for example, that more girls and women are getting involved in games even if what they like to play can be different to the guys.

GAME ON: WOMEN, MEN, AND DUNGEONS

As we have seen, most studies of gender and Internet use suggest that women and men do different things when they go online and boys and men are usually regarded as being much more likely to play games than girls and women (Funk and Buchman 1996; Gorriz and Medina 2000;

Gurer and Camp 2002; Lucas and Sherry 2004). Why is that or even, *is* that still true? Some commentators suggest this is because many (most?) characters in computer games are male (Bryce and Rutter 2003) and where female characters *do* appear, they are often highly sexualized and stereotyped, Lara Croft being a good example, possibly causing female players to reject the character/s and therefore the game (Cassell 2002). Historically, boys and men have always been perceived as the primary target market by games developers, so characters and contexts, especially violent ones, have been constructed with the preferences of a male audience in mind (Laurel 1998), implying that women and men are hardwired to prefer different games styles. However, where comparative research is undertaken, the results produce a much more varied pattern of game playing than this simple binary suggests (see Krotoski 2004). For example, in Hartmann and Klimmt's work, they found that although women in their study disliked sexist and sexualized representations of female characters, they would often sublimate their annoyance in order to enjoy the game overall (2006).

It is, in any case, a rather awkward thing to ask what kinds of games women and men, girls and boys prefer to play, because the answers are likely to be shot through by any number of sociocultural factors associated as much by nurture as nature. It is also important to avoid essentializing so-called female and male traits, as such reductive thinking is unhelpful in understanding the complexity of how we live our lives in the real world let alone in our cyberworlds. Apart from anything else, game players are both embodied gendered subjects but can also play as a differently sexed cyberself, can both spectate and activate, can be both aggressor and victim. Trying to disentangle these different subject positions again leads the researcher up any number of false tracks, ultimately requiring a more nuanced approach. And of course, transferring trend data from one medium (such as arcade or console-based games) to another (such as the Internet) is rarely appropriate, so different are the contexts of different research sites and different research subjects, and so it is with computer games use. Although boys dominate the real-world arcade scene, a recent U.S. study suggests that currently, 44 percent of online games players are female (ESA 2005), which means that whatever we thought we knew about gender-based trends in games participation is challenged when considering the virtual games context.

In a fascinating observational study of girls' computer-based game playing, Carr (2005) provided thirty different kinds of games from which girls could choose to play within the context of a games club. She discovered that game preferences were linked to a number of different factors which were often context and situation specific, depending on player mood, who else was in the room, how close to the top of the choice queue they were, the single- or multiplayer option within the game, the wider popularity of the game, and the look of the game from the cover. Contrary to popular theory, Carr found no evidence that girls were less interested in fight games, and in fact, her participants actively asked for more games in this genre. Nor was there any evidence that aggressive game playing impacted girls' behavior toward each other after their game-playing sessions finished, nor that being competitors on screen influenced the tenor of their offline relationships. A contemporaneous study of young women and men gamers in Germany had very different findings, however, where women expressed little interest in "winning" and lacked confidence in being able to "master" complex game situations (Hartmann and Klimmt 2006). Women in that study much preferred games which produced multilayered, interactive, and sociable environments and in Carr's own study The Sims was also popular with a group of participants. Such a gender-based preference is corroborated elsewhere in the literature, because The Sims requires users to construct a life-world complete with character development and encourages high levels of interaction between players, an environment with which women are more likely to identify than men (Steen et al. 2006).

In Carr's experimental study several games on offer had strong female protagonists but these were rarely chosen by participants, although Carr does not offer an interpretation about why this was so. However, one reading of this preference is that young women prefer to identify with those whom they see as having real power in their real lives (i.e., men) and that to identify with strong women could mark them out as less feminine. This reading complicates a feminist account of women's game playing which argues that women engage in such play as a specific act of resistance to societal norms of femininity (Bryce and Rutter 2003). Good girls don't fight. But what if they pretend to be men and play out the male hero role, what does that say about women's self-identity?

THE INTERNET AS DISCURSIVE SPACE

The ways in which women and men use the Internet is, of course, bound up with how they experience different sites when they are doing more than simply looking for information which does not require an interactive engagement. Some work suggests that one of the reasons why girls and women, when they *do* play games, tend to play single rather than multiuser games is because of the ways in which they are treated once other gamers understand that they are presenting as a female competitor. However, much less competitive environments such as discussion lists also demonstrate gender-based characteristics, which is perhaps not surprising because despite the virtual world into which we plunge when we go online, when we "talk" to others, we are talking to real people, real women and men, even if the ways in which we present ourselves might be very different to how and who we are in our real, offline, lives.

The ways in which communication occurs online has been the subject of considerable academic attention, not least the ways in which the apparently hidden nature of an individual's personal identity encourages a more gender-neutral form of exchange between Net users. The lack of visual cues which suggest either a female or male subject enables the practicing of different kinds of personality to accompany different styles of communication address, allowing the shy to become bold, the nerd to become heroic, and more dangerously, the closet-fantasist to become stalker. One male participant in Dickerson's study of regular Internet users described how much he liked the adoption of an alter ego, saying that "I could be who I wanted to be and no one would be the wiser" (2003, 446). But is the egalitarian free-for-all as democratic and nonhierarchical as some cyberenthusiasts suggest (for example, Bashier 1990; Spender 1995), or does web discourse replicate the same power relations between women and men which exist out there in the real world? Men's communication styles have historically been viewed as being more self-promotional than those of women who tend to be more inclusive, and "male" forms are mostly viewed, by both women and men, as being more powerful (Rondino 1997) and authoritative, even if those same women and men actually *prefer* to experience women's style as it is more caring and collegial.

We have known for a very long time that language is important in challenging or confirming gender stereotypes, that the power to name as other gives the namer (the dominant "we" as opposed to the subordinate "them") power over those who are named. Thus social and every other kind of hierarchy which exists between women and men, as just one dichotomous pair, is reinforced and perpetuated by the use of particular kinds of linguistic strategy, particularly the use of gendered language. Tannen's (1992) work demonstrates that men mostly engage in hierarchical modes of interaction and fix themselves in either a subordinate or superior position in relation to the other person in the communication relationship. Women, on the other hand, tend to approach the world as part of a network with the aim of creating consensus and intimacy. While these are somewhat stereotypical positions in terms of gender traits, Tannen argues that if communication is seen as a continuum, then more men are at the status/hierarchy end and more women are at the community/consensus end. Women tend to make conscious decisions to accept, negotiate, or resist "feminine" modes of communication (Leahy 1994) in ways not dissimilar to Hall's notion of how we "read" cultural texts such as newspapers and TV in these different modes of accept-negotiate-reject (Hall 1997). Unsurprisingly, then, these gender-based communication styles are often carried over into the discursive contexts of the online environment.

But, given the lack of visual cues which mark out speakers as female or male (and thus potentially subverting gender stereotyping and discrimination), does cyber-discourse therefore offer new ways of communicating between women and men which resist traditional power relations? Research findings are, like many other aspects of the Internet, inconclusive on this point, although there is a little less ambiguity in the broad view that gender is a significant differentiator in how women and men *say* they experience online communication. For example, most (but not all) studies of communication practices on the Internet suggest clear gendered attributes in discursive spaces which are dominated by mostly women or mostly men. For example, women-oriented discourse tends toward consensus seeking whereas male discourse tends toward argumentation. Discursive spaces which are more open and mixed often display the more combative male elements which are off-putting to many women (Van Zoonen 2002).

FLAMETHROWERS

Even those of us who do not do much in the way of open chat on the Internet will know about "flaming" and perhaps know women (and men)
who have been victims of this activity. Often, the cloak of anonymity
which is suggested by the Internet encourages overly hostile forms of
communication and, for some users, the lack of visual cues encourages
an even more exaggerated display of gendered discourse; for men this
manifests itself particularly in terms of cyber-machismo tactics such
as flaming (Hall 1996; Thompsen 1996). While undertaking fieldwork
on Internet relay chat (IRC),[1] Bowker (1999) says she was regularly
harassed by other chat roomers who she assumed were male and who
hid their rude displays behind anonymous nicknames. Work on gender
identity in MUDs[2] and other play spaces also demonstrates that individuals presenting as women are much more likely to experience sexual
harassment than those presenting as men (Curtis 1995; McCormick
and Leonard 1996). It is not surprising then that women will often
adopt either gender neutral or male names to avoid such experiences.
In Herring's (1999) comparative work on two discussion forums, she
shows how different operational modes result in different strategies of
harassment. In an IRC, women are "kicked" from the discussion as a
mark of other group members' opprobrium (although they can return
almost immediately), whereas with the academic discussion list she
monitored, participants used language alone to intimidate and silence
women contributors. "In both, male participants advanced views which
were demeaning to women, women responded by resisting the demeaning characteriations and the men then insulted and blamed the women
as the cause of the discord. The ultimate outcome in both cases was that
women complied with male norms or fell silent" (Herring 1999, 151).

Interestingly, although both forums had quite different constituen-
cies and quite different strategies for "rhetorical harassment" to use
Herring's term, the intellectual veneer of the academic discussion list
did not conceal the sexism beneath and in the end worked in precisely
the same way as the more crude and sexualized language used to deni-
grate women participants in the IRC. Crucially for the arguments which
romanticize the potential for subverting gender-based discrimination
through masked identity, Herring makes the point that in "serious"

discussion lists such as those for academic or professional groups, participants are much more likely to use their real identities, thus revealing their gender. Women thus make themselves vulnerable when participating in these kinds of spaces and invite further invective if they challenge the men. Fortunately, the threat of flaming doesn't stop them as this extract from the academic discussion shows.

> I will refrain from responding in kind with generalizations about deficient male logic and hostility etc. I responded in kind to another similar post a while ago just to test my hypothesis: sure enough the rule seems to be that when a male makes nasty, personal, sexist comments, he considers this a demonstration of proper macho aggressiveness. When a female responds in kind, she is hysterical and a man-hater. No surprise there: just checking. (Gail)

What Gail identifies here is the problem which many of us experience, that double standards for women and men are heavily routinized and hard to dislodge. In Dickerson's (2003) study of nurse professionals, she found that although women participants were enthusiastic in using listservs of various practitioner groups, they were often wary about disclosing personal information on open lists such as chat rooms, partly because of suspicion about who might be lurking without speaking. And it is not just individuals who are targeted by hostile users; issue- or gender-specific websites can also be vulnerable. In her work with gender-based equality organizations working in Latin America, Friedman (2003) suggests that fifteen (out of her sample of one hundred) groups said they had experienced some kind of harassment, from strategies of entrapment to being infected with viruses. Some of the lesbian groups in the study mentioned the problem of internal debates (for example, about representation) being leaked into the wider community, and of personal conflicts attracting a wider audience through forwarding e-mails outside an assumed safe space. Such private leaks are scarcely novel or unique to the Internet, but the speed and scope of the Internet means that the possibilities of harm are much greater.

Of course, we should remember that hostile communication is not simply the prerogative of men, since women are more than capable of such behavior, both online and off. In a study of two discussion lists oriented toward women's participation—alt.feminism.individualism and soc.feminism—Fredrick (1999) suggests that sarcasm is often used as an unfriendly tactic. While men will post to these lists as well as women, it is assumed that most of the people who subscribe are women and that the use of sarcasm is a particularly female trait. Other strategies include accusation (hostility) and counterpoint (disagreeing but not abusing the other person), and choosing one strategy over another creates a particular kind of ethos which either welcomes contributions or disinvites further interventions. In a number of the threads she analyzed, Fredrick detects shifts in ethos even within one conversation as different people come in and out, changing the tone as they do so, depending on whether they are collaborating or challenging. This mode of communication is not dissimilar to how people in the real world might behave in terms of the cut and thrust of open discussion. The difference in online communication is that the discussants cannot see each other's nonverbal cues to gauge emotion, so the emotion is often driven up by the language used, often resulting in a much more hostile series of call-and-response than would be likely to happen in a real-time discussion on the same topic. She also notes the use of sexist comments and use of diminutives as put-downs. Interestingly, although both sites purported to be feminist, soc.feminism was seen as more democratic and less hostile, possibly because unlike alt.feminism.individualism, it had a moderator and was thus less likely to tolerate overt hostility.

Part of what Fredrick's work emphasizes is the importance of the moderator in discussion lists and research interest is beginning to turn to issues of chat governance and mediation and speculation about whether the emancipatory possibilities for women on the Net are being realized through their positioning as managers and mediators of online sites. One study which looked at those who control and monitor chat room environments such as IRCs and MUDs found that most controllers were young men with only 25 percent being female, most of whom were generally older than male colleagues (Bowker and Liu 2001). Given the increasing take-up of the Internet by women more generally, how can their small number in decision-making positions be accounted for? One suggestion is a lack of competence and/or confidence in undertaking web activities, which require a high degree of technical knowhow: in the late 1990s, only 13 percent of web managers were women (GVU 1998). It is also possible that women's more consensual style of communication militates against their enthusiastic embrace of a set of tasks which could bring them into conflict with others, given that web managers and chat room operators are expected to monitor their sites and punish miscreants who are abusive.

The use of hostile communication, including flaming, might be seen as merely the latest twist on the old story of male violence against women, operating as a strategy of intimidation intended to silence female voices and discipline female behavior. However, as Scott, Semmens, and Willoughby (1999) point out, although it is certainly unpleasant to be on the receiving end of a flaming assault, such experiences are not typical and most women are not helpless victims of this tactic as we saw from some of the examples above. So it is important to put such behavior into context since it can be counterproductive to overemphasize the negatives for fear of painting cyberspace as an unsafe world where women should fear to tread. We are well advised not to take to the streets on our own after midnight in the real time/space of our real neighborhood, but cyberspace provides numerous tricks by which to shield ourselves from unwanted attention, not all providing 100 percent cover but mostly good enough. Sometimes groups themselves will activate self-policing if they are sufficiently interested in pursuing respectful debate. For example, in Vrooman's (2001) study of a horror fan site, he suggests that members of the group exercise an antiflaming ethos in order to preserve a calm and courteous discursive environment. This is pursued by gentle admonition against hostile voices rather than outright condemnation of the hostile communicator. What appears to take place is the use of encouragement to bring all participants round to a shared vision of what the discussion should be, thus implicitly drawing everyone into a hegemonic practice which has consensual (female?) features.

WOMEN@INTERNET

It is clear from our discussion so far that women and men often do different things when they go online and one of the important aspects of the Internet which is frequently mentioned by women in research studies is the Internet's potential for putting them in touch with other women, especially in terms of sharing information and providing support. As a cyber-enthusiast, Wendy Harcourt (2000, 694) argues that through cyber-networking women are "linking their place-based defense of communities in ways that are challenging public institutional spaces." Harcourt was the powerhouse behind the Women on the Net (WoN) project set up in the 1990s to establish a global network of women and women's organizations. A key characteristic of WoN is the diversity of its members and that many perform multiple roles as community workers, activists, and academics. Part of the discourse between members has been about their shared identity as WoNers and how to project that identity externally (Youngs 1999).

Another of the Internet's enthusiastic supporters, Nicholas Negroponte (1995) argues that the e-generation, for the first time ever, need not obey geographical limits which constrain friendship groups but rather have the entire globe as their potential pool of playmates. His writing, more than a decade ago, was prescient, given the fantastic success of MySpace, YouTube, and Facebook among young people, where users post invitations to come and check out their site, their diary, their blog, their pictures, their music, their friends. Users are knitting themselves rainbow jumpers with varied stitches and patterns with angora and nylon threads in equal measure, with none more important than the other. Interestingly, the Internet is a mostly unmediated and unpoliced space, at least superficially, although we are beginning to understand the extent of online surveillance by government and others and the ways in which our personal details are traded by corporates without our consent. However, notwithstanding the Orwellian aspects of the Internet, a key attraction of the technology is the reality of one person talking to and sharing with many others, unbound by time or geography and united in common interest and purpose.

The heady potential of the Internet, promoted with considerable enthusiasm over the past twenty years, has captured the imagination of tens of millions of us worldwide and has been identified by the global women's movement (as with so many others) as an exciting gateway to enable a genuinely international women's network to develop. In many different contexts and within many different communities of interest, women are "putting information and communication technologies (ICTs) to work for the movement; communicating among dispersed networks, mobilizing action in times of crisis, participating in policy debates and voicing new perspectives" (Gittler 1999, 91). Commenting specifically on global forums such as the Fourth World Conference on Women and NGO[3] Conference in Beijing, 1995, Gittler suggests that by the time the conference was convened, women's groups had already circulated the Platform for Action materials widely, and representatives were thus in a good position to talk authoritatively about what women wanted at and from the conference. Certainly, because of the many eyes, hands, and minds which had scrutinized the draft documentation (and many commentators would never have had such an opportunity to offer input without the use of e-mail), NGOs were often much better informed than their national delegation. Gittler also points out that using electronic communication prior to the conference meant that disparate groups could plan online and then use their attendance at the event itself to more efficient effect. Of course, it wasn't all positive and some of the problems women encountered at that time (and continue to do so) were the expense of Internet connectivity in the developing world, and the vast majority of materials, and indeed Internet sites generally, use English as the primary and often only language. Creative responses to some of these problems have included translation of documents and the repackaging of materials in print and other forms and their dissemination via older technologies such as radio so as to reach wider audiences.

Since the early 1990s when, arguably, women's globally networked political activism really took shape, the number of websites and list-servs focusing on gender issues has risen exponentially and Farwell et al. (1999) argue that the Association for Progressive Communications (APC) has had a crucial role to play in this development through initiatives such as the APC Women's Networking Support Program. The APC is a global network of NGOs which seek to use ICTs to empower and support organizations and individuals to create a better world through, for example, sharing information and enabling global networking. The Women's Networking Support Program has similar purposes to the parent organization but focuses specifically on supporting women and women's organizations through training and networking gateways.

So, how do women link with each other and network for change? Harcourt (2000) provides some highly relevant examples of the ways in which women are using the power of the Internet's global reach to engage an international community with specifically local campaigns, often where women have been targets of government hostility. In this way, local voices are joined by those from the global community, adding a weight and authority which gives considerable strength to women's causes, especially women in the developing world. For example, in India, the Bal Rashmi Society has actively campaigned against culturally entrenched acts of violence against women, such as dowry deaths and domestic abuse. When the society was the subject of a criminal case brought by the Indian government, members used the Internet to publicize the case and received an outpouring of support from individual women and organizations from across the world. Alice Garg from the society says, "We would all have been behind bars had people not rallied to our support" (cited in Harcourt 2000, 695). In Mexico, Claudia Rodriguez was jailed for killing the man who attempted to rape her but was later freed after the campaign organization *Modemmujer* sent out reports of her plight to women's groups all over Latin America and beyond who then campaigned to get Rodriquez freed. These are concrete examples of the Internet's networking capabilities to make a material difference to women's lives.

One extremely ambitious project designed to maximize this aspect of the Internet's many possibilities to empower and connect a global community of women is the Virtual International Women's University (VIFU) project. Since 2000, the project has been bringing hundreds of students, artists, journalists, researchers, and NGO activists together via its website, www.vifu.de. Despite the word *university* in its title, it does not actually provide educational instruction but rather acts as a repository for electronic artifacts (like an e-library) and as a tool for networking. However, it does have its origins in an educational experiment undertaken in Germany in 2000 when the International Women's University facilitated a three-month, face-to-face postgraduate program in which students considered a number of global challenges such as migration, the environment, and health. Once the course finished, the network continued under the name of VIFU. In Zorn's (2004) study of contemporary VIFU participants, she found that although many are alumni of the original program, many others have joined since because of the resources to be found on the site: the majority are students, researchers, and other academics with a smaller number of journalists, politicians, and artists.

Most subscribers are politically active and involved in campaign and other activist groups and networks. At the time of her study, there were participants from more than one hundred countries from all regions of the world. Interestingly and contrary to findings from other studies of gender-based sites, participation from North America is extremely low at around 5 percent and overall more than 50 percent of users are from developing countries. As Zorn points out, understanding the user base was important for the site's development so that low-tech attributes were given preference over flashier components, to make a user-friendly and relatively simple site where downloadable items take up little space and are speedy to deliver.

> What VIFU has done is the empowerment of women through easy access to information. More importantly, it has engendered global solidarity in strengthening personal relationships among activists, academics and change agents the world over. I continue staying connected with human rights lawyers in Africa, with educators in Latin America, with activists and social workers in Asia—all these were possible because VIFU was the technological conduit where life-relationships are nurtured and kept alive. (anonymous participant from the Phillipines/Germany, cited in Zorn 2004, 83)

As we have seen, many women have embraced the potential of the Internet with a passion, using the technology to pursue bold, feminist ends, mostly concerned with global networking and information sharing in what Scott, Semmens, and Willoughby (1999, 547) describe as the "webbed utopia." This description is perhaps a little unfair because these are *not* utopian dreams and fantasies but concrete realities: women-focused sites *do* exist and they *do* perform a valuable function, even if the claims of some enthusiastic cyberfeminists for a global sisterhood are some way from realization (Minahan and Wolfram Cox 2007; Lagesen 2008). But the alliances which the Internet has enabled, between geographically dispersed communities of interest as described above, can and do open up new forums and forms of social and political action, can and do enhance the practice of politics among us as ordinary women, as ordinary citizens (Blair, Gajjalaand and Tulley 2008). Importantly, networks are not formed by some kind of third party "they," but have to be worked at, have to serve a purpose to potential members, have to be created as something of value to which other people want to subscribe. In other words, the Internet does not spontaneously *do* things, but rather, it's what *we* do with the Internet that creates its various cultures, its various networks (May 1998).

WOMEN'S WEB

One very obvious response to the problems of women's exclusion from or harassment in web-based discussion forums has been the creation of women-only spaces by women, for women. Many sites which have this specific focus deliberately subvert traditional renditions of passive femininity in their choice of site name, for example, riotgrrls, geekgrrls, and bitch!, appropriating both masculine terms such as geek but also derogatory terms such as bitch as overt strategies of resistance and clear indicators of a particular political sensibility. Most of these sites are relatively new because the medium is relatively new and because women are only just really beginning to be confident in their use of the more technical aspects of the Internet such as web design.

However, there are a few sites which have been operating for more than ten years including the rather engagingly described Star Fleet Ladies Auxiliary. This mail-based group was set up in 1993 by a group of women who were interested, at least initially, in talking about *Star Trek* without the discursive interventions from prurient young men. In their work with active members of the group, Adams-Price and Chandler (2000) asked women about their experiences of the group and what they got from their membership. Key themes to emerge were that the discussion list constituted a safe space and members were like a family or friendship group interested in nurturing and sharing ideas, thoughts and strategies. Interestingly and unsurprisingly, another theme was that it was *not* about and did not *involve* men. Rather more intriguing was the statement that the site was *not* about *Star Trek*, suggesting that whatever the original motivations were to develop the discussion list, it had transformed itself over time into something else or at least into focusing on something else. It would be interesting to know why, if it is no longer about *Star Trek*, the members maintain their particular list name!

Another website with some years behind it is about-face.org launched in 1997 as a mechanism through which girls could perform rebellion, specifically in relation to the advertising industry's representation of girls and women. In her study of the site, Merskin (2005) suggests that it provides an important forum for what she describes as "Jammer Girls" to post their opinions, their art, and their essays. So, in some ways, the site serves a media literacy function, archiving campaign materials such as complaint letters to companies about ads as examples for potential letter-writing campaigns. How successful this or similar sites are in changing consumer behavior is hard to determine, but as Merskin herself argues, the more such sites promote the active involvement of girls and women to challenge normative renditions of acceptable femininity and, moreover, give them the space and tools to do so, the more likely they will act with their wallets. Posts to the site demonstrate that many girls and young women are entirely conscious of the advertising hype which attends the valorization of the size-zero model and are relieved to find a site that actively encourages rebellion. Given the global reach of the Internet, the potential of such sites to mount a serious challenge to the corporates through, for example, repeating previous stunts such as those carried by the Adbusters site for "Buy Nothing Day" and "TV Turnoff Week," is considerable.

WOMEN AND BLOGS

One of the things that women *do* with the Internet is write up their lives and put them on display via weblogs (blogs) and other kinds of forums such as MySpace and Facebook. Blogs provide important spaces for women (and men) to articulate their hopes and fears, their desires and realities. For women in many countries of the world they represent a uniquely public opportunity to speak up and out, an opportunity mostly denied them within the embodied cultural practices of their everyday life offline, and therefore an undeniably "good" thing (Royal 2008). On the other hand, the lack of translation of this freedom to speak in their real world might actually be counterproductive, throwing into desperate relief the realities of their restricted lives, a state which Newsom (2003) describes as "contained empowerment." This suggests that empowerment is possible but at the level of the individual rather than the wider polity, an empowerment constrained by the existing power hierarchies of online discourses which privilege forms of communication from the North, constrained also by the strategies of gendered subordination which exist for many women in many parts of the world. However, even at the personal level, opportunities to speak, especially beyond the borders of the local, are nevertheless important as Newsom recognizes, and blogs by and for women are a growing Internet phenomenon (Wood 2008). In 2002, there were a thousand-plus sites included in a ring of women webloggers (Hall 2002), although slightly less than 1 percent of all these forums were marked out as originating and hosted by women in the South. One reason might be that free speech in many countries is as controlled on the Internet as it is in more traditional media with "subversives" traced by sophisticated tracking and online surveillance, and then punished (Newsom and Lengel 2003).

FLAMETHROWERS, AGAIN

While these women-flavored sites offer many benefits to women subscribers, they also generate various unfriendly reactions. Responses from men to women-only sites or women-focused discussions are often hostile, arguably aimed (again) at intimidating women into silence and/ or withdrawal. One woman who authors her own e-zine comments, "I've been surprised at the aggressive response from certain men to a women-only site. I've had quite a lot of e-mails actually accusing me of sexism and men-hating. Some of the messages are really unpleasant and offensive. . . . From other women I've spoken to I think this is a fairly typical experience" (anon. participant cited in Cresser, Gunn, and Balme 2001, 461). Thus the safe space offered to women by women-only sites can on the one hand be viewed as empowering to the women who frequent and use such spaces for networking, support, and information sharing, but simultaneously can invite attack from men who are annoyed by their exclusion from even the smallest area of the vast electronic kingdom which is the World Wide Web. The question we should ask, then, given that the great majority of Internet-based research makes clear that both women and men view the medium as essentially male and dominated by men and male concerns, is why men feel they must challenge the existence of those relatively few spaces which women have constructed just for themselves? Why do men feel they should be able to access anything, anytime, anywhere, anyhow? The cloak of invisibility offered by the Internet means that men can pose as women (and vice versa) and get inside these spaces of female solidarity and create their mischief. But women are getting wise to these kinds of tactics and are developing ever more sophisticated gatekeeping mechanisms including password protection and other safeguard devices to try and maintain the safe space women want. Fortunately, most women who are regular contributors to and developers of websites such as e-zine publishers are not fazed by negative feedback and will often, instead, rise to the challenge of encouraging more women to get online and become active agents rather than passive consumers. One such strategy is to provide links from e-zines to web authoring sites as well as sharing good practice and hints and tips on how to produce good material. In this, albeit small way, women actively encourage each other to have a more visible presence and voice on the Internet (Cresser, Gunn, and Balme 2001).

ENGENDERING THE DIGITAL DIVIDE

So far much of the discussion has focused on differences between women and men in terms of how they experience the Internet and what they do when they go online, but such discussions are predicated on a notion that individuals have relatively easy access to a computer and therefore the Internet, often in the comfort of a technically sophisticated home or office. These discussions are often threaded with words like "rights" and "access," but despite the political intent behind these liberal discussions, using the language of rights places this discourse firmly within a Western paradigm because there is an implicit assumption of preexisting skills such as literacy (Agustin, 1999). The education of girls is not seen as a high priority in many traditional societies, so the subsequent take-up of Internet services by women is much lower than men, differences exacerbated by rural-urban divisions as well as endemic poverty. There is often an implicit assumption that membership of the wired world is a desirable goal of *all* the world's peoples, an assumption which needs to be balanced against the fact that two-thirds of the world's population has never even made a phone call (Bautista 1999). Despite significant infrastructural developments across the globe which means that we can talk about the global village with a bit more confidence, the digital divide between North and South, the haves and the have-nots, is still very much in evidence. The problem of differential access to and use of popular media is not a new one and contemporary arguments about exclusion and control in relation to the Internet were similarly rehearsed during the early days of the printing press. Then, as now, it was recognized that those who control media output and those who have the knowledge to use (new) technology are in a considerably more powerful position than those who do not. As computer skills are increasingly becoming an essential rather than a merely desirable attribute in the global marketplace, so their lack (more prevalent among women than men in all regions of the world) is likely to become a major impediment to future employment opportunities (Wakunuma 2007).

Although every year the digital divide (at least in crude, hardware terms) becomes a little narrower as ever more remote and developing regions of the world get connected, we can still talk of a considerable technological underclass. Two interesting and empirically-based studies of the Internet in Africa (Nyabuga 2007; Wakunuma 2007) show that although parts of Africa, in this case Kenya and Zambia, are witnessing a significant growth in the uptake of Internet services, such users are still much more likely to be living in the metropolitan conurbations than the rural areas where the majority of African communities actually live. Importantly, what both studies show is that when asked and when they understood the meaning of the Internet, ordinary citizens were enthusiastic about the technology and its empowering potential. Chalaby (2000) points out that new media are often associated with the promise of new freedoms through advocacy and the promotion of liberty, and the Internet is no exception. But as the participants in Nyabuga and Wakunuma's respective research projects pointed out, although people recognized the importance of the Internet in the digital future, choosing between buying food or sending an e-mail was a no-brainer.

Despite rhetorical statements which claim a desire to enfranchise women to the digital knowledge economy, the very context of Africa itself as a developing region beset by numerous political and economic problems, as well as deeply mired in traditional cultures which routinely subordinate women, makes enactment problematic. "As Africa's women struggle to enlarge their spheres of influence in political, economic and social arenas, the question is whether the Internet and other digital technologies will become agents of transformation or reproduce the inequalities of the status quo" (Robins 2002, 235). Robins's question is a good one and the few studies which have explored it at an empirical rather than simply theoretical level have tended to suggest that the Internet is simultaneously both a good and a not-so-good thing. In other words, the same kinds of ambivalences around benefits/disadvantages exist in Africa as elsewhere, but where variables in the debate around the digital divide such as gender and class are exaggerated because of the strong double grip of patriarchy and greed. A good example of these ambiguities can be seen in Robins's study of gender-based ICT projects in Senegal where she identified a variety of initiatives aimed at encouraging women's take-up of ICT, ranging from computer training for rural women to paying for Internet access by a woman entrepreneur to source haute couture for her wealthy clientele (2002). But overall she argues that the most significant beneficiaries of the Internet revolution in Senegal are a small group of the already privileged, urban elite, the already-haves. The have-nots continue in their disadvantaged state and the have-somethings might get a little something extra, but rarely something sustainable.

As the developing world liberalizes its telecommunications sector and encourages a free market and international trade, so countries become susceptible to the blandishments of organizations which might not always share the development vision (Robins 2002; Nyabuga 2007). Such opening up of the sector is usually a key demand of donor organizations before they are willing to provide aid and assistance, but in much of Africa part of the trade-off has been a cut in funding for education and health care services (Wakunuma 2007) because prioritization of resources is, in the end, a zero-sum game. But it's hard to see how the U.N.'s Millennium Development Goals to build the Global Information Society and wire the world can be better achieved by reducing the number of village schools. "Will knowledge, information and communication . . . really feed people, close the gap between the rich and the poor and solve problems where other development strategies have failed?" (Zorn 2004, 76).

Although U.N.-inspired strategies such as the African Information Society Initiative attempt to provide developing-world friendly ways of getting people online—for example, through the setting up of telecenters in villages rather than wiring every home—such centers tend to be run and frequented by men, prompting calls to reexamine exactly who benefits from such initiatives, which tend to be the most popular type of technology-aid gifting by Western donor organizations (Huyer 1997; Fontaine 2000; Wakunuma 2007). So instead of empowering women, the ways in which ICTs are *actually* developing in much of Africa serves to reinforce traditional (patriarchal) power relations between women and men. The ways in which technologies are controlled by global players means that linking the world via global networks serves to also reinforce the power relations between North and South, constituting a contemporary form of colonial control and rule.

Thus, there are any number of contradictions provoked in the surrender to technology's seductive embrace, where individuals, NGOs, and governments all agree that people (women and men) *must* get involved in ICTs in general and the Internet in particular so as to get plugged into the knowledge economy and be globally competitive. But then inadequate infrastructure, poverty, the impulse of global capital, and the conglomeratization of global media all militate strongly against genuine empowerment for Africa and the other developing regions of the world. As women in African and other traditional societies are yoked by considerably lower status than men, they are disadvantaged twice, once by the internal problems of patriarchy and again by the external forces of global capital (see also Heeks 1999; Robins 2002). The point to understand here is that although the hardware of technology might be gender neutral, its appropriation and use certainly is not. This discussion has focused on Africa as typical of a developing region, but the same arguments can also be made of other contexts such as India or even Eastern Europe, as those regions also struggle to become part of the global village but face many of the same problems of access, connectivity, and poverty (Lengel 1998).

However, all is not only doom and gloom and there are any number of individual studies which look at individual cases and find something positive to say. For example, Mbambo (1999) suggests that although not quite yet a mass medium, the Internet is becoming a popular means by which to disseminate socially useful information such as that relating to health issues through dedicated websites, e-mail, and listservs. However, she also points out that much of the information which is being consumed and/or downloaded by African users in Africa tends to be generated from outside the continent. This situation must be addressed if Africa is to become the architect of its own development rather than subject to Eurocentric perspectives on development, which may have absolutely no relevance or resonance with African communities themselves. It is also important for the technology's survival that content is relevant and useful in order that users will bother to go online and find it.

The enormous potential of the Internet to change the lives of people across the world is, undoubtedly, a cause for celebration and we should welcome those concrete activities and actions which progress women's empowerment in particular. But we must also be vigilant in maintaining our concern for the material conditions of women's lives, which are often so harsh as to render redundant the very notion of women in the wired world. Crucially, we need to understand the inscription of gender in technology and look at the relationship between women, culture, technology, and development in order to identify the needs and desires which lie within the interstices of these concepts. This would then enable mapping out an agenda for change which could be genuinely empowering for women and men in the developing world.

GENDER AND THE INTERNET— REASONS TO BE CHEERFUL OR FEARFUL?

As with everything else associated with the Internet, enthusiasm for its positive potential is matched by pessimism about its potential abuse, and in between is concern about the actual harm caused to users by doing too much computer-mediated communication (CMC). Chief among these concerns is the propensity toward loneliness, depression (Jackson et al. 2001), and social isolation. Some commentators have researched what they describe as Net addiction, which causes sufferers to neglect their friends, cease engagement with the real world, and retreat into a virtual space where all communication is disembodied fantasy speak (Young 2008). The implication here is that Net-based friendships and communication are inherently less satisfying than physical ones and those who prefer them are social inadequates who can't get the real thing. Given researchers' preoccupation with naming things, the phenomenon of Internet addiction is now described as pathological Internet use (PIU; Morahan-Martin and Schumacher 2000). Any number of experimental studies provide support for this fear, arguing that within a given sample population those individuals who are deemed to be more socially anxious and lonely are more likely to believe that the Internet is more controllable, provides better feedback and a deeper and richer environment than their less anxious peers. Importantly, more anxious users also believe that the Internet is more rewarding than face-to-face communication, and boys and young men are often seen as more involved in and more enamored of computer-mediated communication than girls and young women, especially in their use of interpersonal interactions such as chat rooms and multiplayer games (Young 1998; Morahan-Martin and Schumacher 2000; Caplan 2005; Jochen, Valkenburg and Schouten 2005).

Girls and women are regarded as more vulnerable online users than boys and while teenagers of both sexes have indicated that they have indeed been approached by strangers online (Lenhart, Rainie, and Lewis 2001)—and sites like MySpace and Facebook actively encourage casual networking and friendship development—very few seem concerned about the possible dangers involved, possibly because of a widely acknowledged youthful perception of invincibility. For some commentators, then, the enthusiastic embrace of the Internet as a space in which women could finally fulfill their potential—the battle cry of cyberfeminists such as Dale Spender (1995), Sherry Turkle (1995) and Sadie Plant (1997) in the 1990s—must be balanced by a more sober, empirically informed and critical consideration of the Internet's influence in and impact on our contemporary lives. What made those early feminist interventions into Internet analysis so committed to the notion of the Web's woman-friendly proclivities was precisely the Net/working aspect of the Internet, that is, that woman were (and are) really good at networking and communication and here was a medium which encouraged both. Wonderful. Finally, a girl's own story. And it is easy to see the attraction of such a proposition. As feminism itself was experiencing a media-generated backlash in the 1990s, finding a place to call one's own, and one, moreover, whose techno-militaristic provenance and historical exclusion of women could be hijacked for good, feminist ends, must have been incredibly exciting.

But it is clear that the Internet is *still* a highly contested space in terms of gender identity, with claims of its specific feminine (communication) or masculine (technology) character being challenged by a middle ground of gender fluidity. Van Zoonen (2002) provides a useful discussion in attempting to understand the articulation between gender and the Internet by invoking three dimensions of gender which are used to test the relationship. *Gender as social construction* supports the idea that the Internet is male because most owners, designers, and workers within the ICT sector are men (see also Haddon 1999). The perception of the Internet as male is borne out not just by the statistics on ICT as an occupational category dominated by men but also in terms of how young people view a career in the industry. One large-scale web-based survey of nearly three thousand young women and men discovered that while 60 percent of young men wanted to work in technology, only 26 percent of young women had similar desires (cited in Singh 2001, 409). *Gender as symbol* also supports the notion of a male-framed Internet as so many texts and practices are deemed to be masculine. *Gender as identity* partially supports the argument that the Internet is female because of the community- and network-building and consensus-seeking aspects, but this is a much weaker claim than the other two. "As with science, the very language of technology, its symbolism, is masculine. . . . Therefore to enter this world, to learn its language, women have first to forsake their femininity" (Wajcman 1991, 19).

In the end, Van Zoonen suggests that these various claims for an Internet which is feminine, masculine, or beyond gender must be linked to the ways in which the Internet is conceptualized as a cultural object or a mode of constructed communication. In other words, what does the Internet actually mean to the individuals who use it? In her own study of Internet use among Dutch couples, Van Zoonen found that there were four media cultures in play: traditional (predominant use by male partner, lack of confidence by female partner); deliberative (shared use and interest but often man's use is viewed as more important); individualized (equal careers and individualized adaptation, e.g., bringing home a laptop); and reverse IT (woman makes much greater use but only because of a lack of male interest). Singh's very similar study in Australia showed quite different results, indicating that women who used the Internet at work did not want to come home and spend further hours in front of a screen (2001), which was the reason given by some of the men in Van Zoonen's reverse IT media culture for giving over the computer to their female partner. While Van Zoonen argues that women will *consciously* withdraw from computer use because it contradicts normative self-perceptions of femininity, Singh's work shows that they will also avoid using the computer after work as a way of clearly marking out leisure time for themselves.

The Internet is still evolving and the ways in which we access this technology have already moved beyond the boundary of the PC, to mobile phones and PDAs. What we do with the Internet as women and men, how we use it, and for what purposes are also constantly evolving. Come back in five years time and let's have this discussion again, but I'm pretty sure we will have different things to say.

FURTHER READING

Harcourt, W. ed. (1999). *Women@Internet: Creating New Cultures in Cyberspace*. London and New York: Zed Books.

Mazzarella, S. R., ed. (2005). *Girl Wide Web: Girls, the Internet and the Negotiation of Identity*. New York: Peter Lang.

Negroponte, N. (1995). *Being Digital*. London: Hodder & Staughton.

Turkle, S. (1995). *Life on the Screen: Identity in the Age of the Internet*. London: Weidenfield and Nicholson.

Wakeford, N. (2002). *Networks of Desire: Gender, Sexuality and Computing Culture*. London and New York: Routledge.

6

ENDPOINT

Representation of the world, like the world itself, is the work of men; they describe it from their own point of view, which they confuse with the absolute truth.

—Simone de Beauvoir[1]

With current magazines full of ad campaigns featuring older celebrities and models—40-year-old Helena Christensen for Agent Provocateur and 52-year-old Jerry Hall for Chanel—tackling other issues such as race, weight and airbrushing seemed the logical next step for magazine editorials. And this month French Elle offers three different covers of Monica Bellucci, Sophie Marceau and Eva Herzigova shot without make-up and image retouching. While these covers and advertisements cannot erase the message that is sent to women by the typical images of perfection, they do show an alternative. (Fisher 2009, 22)

At the beginning of this book, I suggested that discussions about gender and media would, almost of necessity, include a discussion about power and control, about patriarchy and capital, about the corporates and the rest of us. As I hope I have shown in the preceding pages, the ways in which women and men function in society, how we behave, what we believe, how we are different, and how we are the same are rooted in both our own experiences and personal dispositions but also influenced by what we see around us in society, in culture, and in the media. While we may no longer be cultural dupes or couch potatoes or easy targets for political propaganda, nor are we entirely immune from the blandishments of the media to consume particular products, wear particular labels, look a certain way, desire a certain lifestyle. Most of our lives, at least in the developed but also increasingly the developing nations too, are irrevocably entwined with media of different kinds accessed via a number of routes, from the humble radio, to the TV, computer, movie theater, Internet, mobile phone, PDA, and so on. It is possible to live a 24/7 media-saturated existence, catching up with news on demand, watching TV shows an hour after they were first broadcast, downloading a favorite radio program directly onto your iPod.

Given the media-saturated nature of our contemporary world, it is hard to sustain an argument which says that we are so media savvy, so media literate, that we can always detect when we are being played. But the question to ask is, so what? Why do issues of gender matter in a context where we have had three decades of equality legislation, where a woman was a serious prospect to become president of the United States, where Oprah is one of the richest women in the world? Because these gender-flavored phenomena are matched by escalating incidences of domestic violence against women, by increasing numbers of women with eating disorders, by a burgeoning demand for cosmetic surgeons to give breast implants to adolescent girls as a birthday present from their parents. The extent to which the positives and negatives of women's progress and subordination can be attributed to the whims of the media is impossible to say but I argue that there *is* an effect whether we care to acknowledge it, regardless of the force or direction of that effect. So, in attempting to pull together the strands of the various arguments which have been made so far, let us consider what the preceding pages tell us about the state of play between gender and media and the myriad ways in which the nuances of that relationship play out in the real world of real women and men.

A key issue which threads through several of the topics we have covered here has been the ways in which women and men are differently represented in popular media discourse. In particular, despite the gains which *have* been made in recognizing the complexity of meanings connoted by terms such as *femininity* and *masculinity*, sex-based stereotypes demonstrate a remarkable resilience. In some ways, one of the great triumphs of the advertising industry, as exemplary purveyors of iconic images of corporeal perfection, is the clever insistence that the resexualization of women's bodies, especially by women themselves, is evidence of feminist achievement and of women's enhanced place in the world. That encouraging men to take care of their bodies (albeit through their consumption of expensive grooming products, natch) is a sign of the leveling out of difference between the sexes. To raise a voice in protest at this joyful celebration of porno-chic is to open oneself to the charge of cultural dinosaur, of being out of step with the post-ironic, post-modern, post-feminist zeitgeist: hey, sister, get with the program!

But critiques of advertising are not always and everywhere about women (or men) as victim in persistent thrall to the media's bodily prescription of ideal beauty. At one very important level, women's more assertive response to advertising's tyranny of identikit beauty, by stretching "Porn Star" over less than perfect 34E breasts or revealing a rather more lumpy midriff or buttock cleavage than Kate Moss, is to be welcomed for its refusal to be cowed into sackcloth by the perpetual circulation of airbrushed fantasy. But the problem for feminism is the (seeming) lack of any political consciousness to accompany these acts of insolent pride. While the media can pretend that women and men are now equal, that women really can have it all and be both feminine and successful, *pace* (apparently) Paris Hilton, most women themselves seem unaware that they are practicing some kind of kick-ass assertive womanhood, instead seeing themselves as just being, well, themselves, no politics in sight, feminist or otherwise. The resexualization of women's bodies as objects in popular culture and the simultaneous framing of women as possessing autonomous and sexy subjecthood produces a weird clash of ideology, where women both objectify themselves for external (men's?) consumption but simultaneously frame themselves as exemplifying grrl power. Sisters are doing it for themselves, but for others too?

What most men's lifestyle magazines sell is a version of masculinity which is young, white, ripped, and beautiful. Even as the male audience for these texts acknowledge the impossibility of achieving that look for themselves, they nevertheless buy into the image in much the same way as women. Recognizing the sly deceit of the digitally enhanced jawline or sexily sweaty six-pack does not detract from the subsequent purchase of protein shakes or tinted moisturiser, especially when endorsed by celebrity athletes. But, if women and men are just pleasing themselves, making choices because *they* want to, not because they are told to, or manipulated into, then why is there such a strong sense of identikit beauty for women and men? Why does my twenty-year-old niece and her friends all wear hair extensions, heavy make-up, posh-slut clothes, and exist, seemingly, only on rice cakes and Evian? Why does my twenty-three-year-old nephew and his chums go to the gym after work to help each other pump ever heavier iron, relaxing afterward with a protein-packed smoothie and a few cans? I hate sounding like my mother and at some level what I describe here is nothing so very new, but what *is* new is the idea that somehow these trends signal liberation. I beg to differ and suggest that, on the contrary, this crop of sexy identities, although given totemic value as the touchstone of our contemporary autonomy, actually conceal the manufactured nature of this not-so-emancipated subjecthood. It's about the money, stupid.

So much for entertainment, but what of the ways in which women are represented in factual media? Is the situation any rosier, at a time when women are holding the reins of political power in several countries, voted in by publics who believe that women's leadership is not only significantly different to that of men but could actually effect change for the better? Sadly, what an analysis of women's representation in news demonstrates, incontrovertibly, is that the media's framing (in every sense of the word) of women remains highly restricted and mostly negative in ways which are not simply the consequence of the idiosyncrasies of this newspaper or that TV channel or that radio station but rather appears to be a *global* phenomenon which has endured over time and across media formats, and continues to do so. Women feature most often when they are in the most pain, when they are the victim, broken, dead, or when they are the wives, daughters, or girlfriends of newsworthy men. Even when women of significance do manage to attract the media's attention, journalists still manage to find ways to undermine their potency as agents of their own destiny. On December 27, 2007, the former prime minister of Pakistan, Benazir Bhutto, was assassinated and in the succeeding days countless column inches were devoted to an analysis of her political career and the implications of her death. The BBC correspondent Owen Bennett Jones demonstrates precisely the unrealistic expectations which bedevil women politicians and the ways in which journalistic discourse is gender inflected. We might ask ourselves, would the following sentiments be uttered if Bhutto had been male? "So—Benazir Bhutto was domineering, articulate, brave, charismatic, good fun, quite flirtatious, very cynical and she was flawed. Tens of millions of Pakistanis—illiterate and impoverished—looked to her with hope, faith and even love. She failed them" (Bennett Jones 2007, n.p.). Even taking the most generous view of the media's role in the articulation of a normative social world order which privileges men and male concerns over those of women, that is, that they do it unwittingly, it is nonetheless irresistible to suggest that there must be *some* element of complicity, some sense of collusion with the circulation of words and pictures which routinize what it is to be female and male in contemporary society.

In an interview after church services in Bowling Green on Sunday, [Hillary] Clinton for the first time addressed what women have been talking about for months, what she refers to as the "sexist" treatment she has endured at the hands of the pundits, media and others. The lewd T-shirts. The man who shouted "Iron my shirt" at a campaign event. The references to her cleavage and her cackle. "It's been deeply offensive to millions of women. . . . I believe this campaign has been a groundbreaker in a lot of ways. But it certainly has been challenging given some of the attitudes in the press, and I regret that, because I think it's been really not worthy of the seriousness of the campaign and the historical nature of the two candidacies we have here. . . . The manifestation of some of the sexism that has gone on in this campaign is somehow more respectable, or at least more accepted, and . . . there should be equal rejection of the sexism and the racism when it raises its ugly head. . . . It does seem as though the press at least is not as bothered by the incredible vitriol that has been engendered by the comments by people who are nothing but misogynists." (Romano 2008, C01)

So far, so mixed when considering the interplay between gender and media in traditional media, but what about new technologies? To what extent can we look to the Internet to restructure gender relations in more equitable ways and enable women and men to reach their full potential in the heady atmosphere of cyberspace? Well, as with our analyses of other media, the picture here is similarly complicated, similarly contradictory. As with everything else associated with the Internet, enthusiasm for its positive potential is matched by pessimism about its potential abuse, and in between is concern about the actual harm caused to users by doing too much CMC (computer-mediated communication). Girls and women are regarded by many researchers to be more vulnerable to the negative aspects of online life, not least because of their greater propensity to get involved in real-time meetings with people they have only met on the Internet. While there are any number of horror stories about "what happened next," the rise in social networking sites such as Facebook and significant developments in online dating sites suggests that despite the caution about stranger danger, many people regard the Internet as a viable space through which to meet real people.

Although most research suggests that the contours of the digital divide which separate the haves from the have-nots reflect the same kinds of divisions which exist throughout society, including the gender-shaped ones, new technologies nonetheless offer unique opportunities for women's emancipation. Websites for women dissolve geographical and temporal boundaries and foster networking and support for a global sisterhood and the use of the Internet for global advocacy has meant that the dire situation of women (and men) in many areas of the developing world is evidenced to a world community who can, in turn, petition their disgust.

As is clear, then, although there are many aspects of the gender-media relation which continue to be extremely problematic, the situation is not one of abiding gloom, and importantly, women have not stood idly by but have campaigned, acted up, and pushed forward with reforms which have impacted on media organizations, both in terms of representation but also in relation to workplace cultures. In my own work with Carolyn Byerly in which we interviewed ninety women media workers in twenty nations, we mapped the ways in which women have been active in challenging the hegemony of the media industry in our development of a model of women's activism, what we have called the Model of Women's Media Action, which incorporates the notion of pathways (Byerly and Ross 2006). The first path, Politics to Media, relates to women's decision to incorporate media work as part of their wider political activism through their production of creative artifacts. Women following this path acquired media skills as they went along so that they could produce media such as newsletters, or radio shows or websites. The second path—Media Profession to Politics—was taken by women already working within mainstream media organizations who decided to use their insider position to effect change from within. Women who followed the third path, Advocate Change Agent, used a range of strategies to bring pressure on media organizations to improve the ways in which women are treated. Invariably, this included research and analysis about women and media, including publication of reports or articles, or it may have been to mobilize people to write letters or take some other action; women following this path were often involved in NGOs which have a specific gender advocacy purpose. The fourth and final path, Women-owned Media, included those women who struck out to control media through the establishment of specific, women-focused media companies, including book and magazine publishing, syndicated radio programming, women's news agencies, and independent film and video companies.

Women's agency, manifested through their media activism, shows what can be achieved through deliberate and conscious action, defining the contours of struggle over women's right to communicate, and then overcoming them. Significantly, this struggle is not fixed or immutable but rather is a shared experience and endeavor, fought by many over continents and across time. The Model of Women's Media Action we developed incorporates the thoughts and strategies of many media-active women and reveals the hidden *her*story of women's involvement in the change agenda. Importantly, it recuperates women's agency and successes and shows how they have created the spaces to come to voice both within mainstream media but also in the development of alternative and independent media. Many of us are in for the long haul, recognizing that although the glass is half-full, it is simultaneously half-empty as well. The Fourth World Conference on Women, which took place in Beijing in September 1995, included among its strategic objectives, "To increase the participation and access of women to expression and decision making in and through the media and new technologies of communication" (United Nations, 1996, Strategic Objective J.1). One of its calls on global governments was to "support research into all aspects of women and the media so as to define areas needing attention and action and review existing media policies with a view to integrating a gender perspective." I hope that through the pages of this book, I have made a contribution to this laudable but challenging objective, generating a deal of heat and hopefully also a little light. Unlike some of my feminist foremothers who in recent times have recanted their former politics in favor of a postmodern sensibility which rehearses the anything-goes philosophy with terrifying complacency, I am happy to use the *F* word. Viva Viragos!

> The G-spot is in the ears. He who looks for it below there is wasting his time. —Isabel Allende

NOTES

CHAPTER 1

1. *Loaded* was launched in the United Kingdom in 1994, targeted at young men (the lad) with unapologetic interest in sex, drink, and football and has been seen by some commentators as one of the key cultural influences of the 1990s.

2. *FHM* is the best-selling magazine of any kind in Europe and has the largest circulation of any magazine in the United Kingdom (National Readership Survey, quoted in Rogers 2005).

3. *Top Gear* was the top car show on U.K. television for many years, recently rebranded as *Fifth Gear* when the show moved to a different channel but still resolutely framed for the "boy racer" audience. It is a studio-based show and purports to be consumer focused, including test drives of new cars, interviews with celebrity car owners, couch-based interviews with guests, and so on.

4. For example, he infamously described Judaism as a "gutter religion" and Adolf Hitler as "a great man" (Kotzin 1994, 224).

CHAPTER 2

1. These campaigns are discussed in more detail later in this chapter.

2. Jamie's School Dinners, at www.channel4.com/life/microsites/J/jamies _school_dinners/index.html.

3. See, for example, Campbell and Asthana, 2007.

4. uk.news.yahoo.com/skynews/20070711/tuk-calls-for-ban-on-under-16
-models-45dbed5.html (accessed November 26, 2007).

5. For Him Magazine.

6. The debate around "page 3" is that the United Kingdom's most popular
tabloid, the *Sun*, has featured a topless woman model on page 3 of the newspaper for the last thirty years, defiant in the face of numerous challenges for
page 3 to be consigned to the trash bin of bad taste, but still it keeps going, now
joined by others such as the *Sunday Sport*.

7. To see the poster, go to www.johnriviello.com/bodyimage/ruby.html.

8. campaignforrealbeauty.co.uk/whitepaper.asp (accessed November 30,
2007).

9. campaignforrealbeauty.co.uk/dsef07/t5.aspx?id=8120 (accessed November 30, 2007).

10. The statement denoting the road directions to the Motor Show venue.

CHAPTER 3

1. Unsurprisingly, detractors of the availability of sexually explicit material
have no difficulty in defining exactly what pornography is and is not—see later
discussion.

2 In the early days of the magazine, most photographs had originally been
taken for the gay men's magazine market.

3. The festival was designed to be a forum in which "netporn" could be both
discussed but also enjoyed, without the connotations of sexual perversion which
often attends such debates. www.networkcultures.org/clickme/

4. For the purposes of this chapter, I have *only* been discussing the circulation and consumption of materials that are legal to own, download, purchase,
or view.

5. Candida Royalle was a porn star before becoming a (porn) filmmaker.

CHAPTER 4

1. The passing into common currency of the British term *WAGs* to describe
the wives and girlfriends of footballers and other celebrities demonstrates
perfectly the tabloid turn in journalism, with coverage of the exploits of this or

that WAG easily displacing news of a catastrophic hurricane in Bangladesh as the lead item.

2. www.whomakesthenews.org.

3. www.genderlinks.org.za.

4. Amongst other things, Genderlinks performs a 'mediawatch' function in terms of monitoring South African media and the ways in which women are portrayed.

5. Much of this section is informed by the results of interviews I conducted with women parliamentarians from Britain (1995, 2000, 2006), Australia (1998), South Africa (1999), Northern Ireland (2002, 2006), and New Zealand (2007).

6. Women in Journalism are a group of British women journalists who got together in 1999 to provide support and information exchange.

7. For explorations of women newsworkers' experiences in different national contexts and the kinds of strategies they adopt to cope, see de Bruin and Ross (2004) and Robinson (2005).

8. Personal telephone interview with Thandazo (not her real name), a black woman journalist who worked for a major newspaper, June 18, 2003.

9. In 1981, Craft was hired by the station and within six months she was reassigned away from news on the grounds that focus group research on her performance suggested that she was "too old, too unattractive, and not sufficiently deferential to men" (cited in Chambers, Steiner, and Fleming 2004, 140). Craft filed a lawsuit, and although the trial jury awarded her $500,000 on the basis that there had been sex discrimination and hiring fraud, an appellate judge reversed the decision and despite numerous further efforts to have the case reheard, Craft was ultimately unsuccessful.

10. www.bitchmagazine.com (accessed October 11, 2007).

11. Interview with Judy Sandison, SABC, June 8, 2003; e-mail correspondence with Judy Sandison, May 10, 2004.

CHAPTER 5

1. IRC is a virtual, multiuser, multichannel real-time chat forum in which users log on using their nicknames.

2. MUDs (multiuser dungeons) are spaces for multiuser games that individuals enter using a password and participate as a virtual self (avatar) that may not resemble their real selves.

3. Nongovernmental organization.

CHAPTER 6

1. Simone de Beauvoir quotes. About.com, womenshistory.about.com/od/quotes/a/de_beauvoir.htm (accessed April 25, 2009).

REFERENCES

Aalberg, T., and Jenssen A. T. (2007). Gender stereotyping of political candidates: An experimental study of political communication. *Nordicom Review* 28(1): 17–32.

Adams, D. (2000). Can pornography cause rape? *Journal of Social Philosophy* 31(1): 1–43.

Adams-Price, C. E., and Chandler, S. (2000). Star Fleet Ladies Auxiliary: Evolution of an online women's mailing list. *CyberPsychology & Behavior* 3(5): 811–30.

Agustin, L. (1999). They speak but who listens? In W. Harcourt, ed., *Women@Internet: Creating New Cultures in Cyberspace*, 149–55. London and New York: Zed Books.

Alexander. S. H. (1999). Messages to women on love and marriage from women's magazines. In M. Myers, ed., *Mediated Women: Representations in Popular Culture*, 25–38. Cresskill, N.J.: Hampton Press.

Allan, S. (1999). *News Culture*. Buckingham: Open University Press.

———. (2004). *News Culture*, 2nd ed. Maidenhead, U.K.: Open University Press.

———. ed. (2005). *Journalism: Critical Issues*. Maidenhead, U.K.: Open University Press.

Alloo, F. (1999). Information technology and cyberculture: The case of Zanzibar. In W. Harcourt, ed., *Women@Internet: Creating New Cultures in Cyberspace*, 156–61. London and New York: Zed Books.

American Psychiatric Association. (2000). *Diagnostic and Statistical Manual of Mental Disorders*, 4th ed. Washington, D.C.: American Psychiatric Association.

Amon, M. (2008, August 31). For some local women, it's wait and see for Palin. Newsday.com.

Anderson, C. A., and Bushman, B. J. (2001). Effects of violent video games on aggressive behavior, aggressive cognition, aggressive affect, physiological arousal and prosocial behavior: A meta-analytic review of the scientific literature. *Psychological Science* 12: 353–59.

Annenberg Public Policy Center. (2002). *No Room at the Top?* Philadelphia: University of Pennsylvania Press.

Ansolabehere, S., Behr, R., and Iyengar, S. (1991). Mass media and elections: An overview. *American Politics Quarterly* 19: 109–39.

Association for Progressive Communications [APC]. (1997). Global Networking for Change: Experiences from the APC Women's Programme, Survey Findings. London: APC.

Appleyard, B. (2000, December 4). Goodbye to the dirty mac image. *New Statesman*, 10, 12.

Arizpe, L. (1999). Freedom to create: Women's agenda for cyberspace. In W. Harcourt, ed., *Women@Internet: Creating New Cultures in Cyberspace*, xii–xvi. London and New York: Zed Books.

Armstrong, C. L. (2004). The influence of reporter gender on source selection in newspaper stories, *Journalism and Mass Communication Quarterly* 81(1): 139–54.

Atkeson, L.R. (2009). Not all cues are created equal: the conditional impact of female candidates on political engagement. *Journal of Politics* 65(4): 1040-1061

Attorney General's Commission on Pornography (1986), *Final Report*. Washington, DC Department of Justice.

Attwood, F. (2002). A very British carnival: Women, sex and transgression in *Fiesta* magazine. *European Journal of Cultural Studies* 5(1): 91–105.

———. (2004). Pornography and objectification. *Feminist Media Studies* 4(1): 7–19.

Barthes, R. (1973). *The Fashion System*. New York: Hill & Wang.

Bartkowski, J. P. (2001). Breaking walls, raising fences: Masculinity, intimacy and accountability among the Promise Keepers. In R. H. Williams, ed., *Promise Keepers and the New Masculinity: Private Lives and Public Morality*, 33–72. Lanham, Md.: Lexington Books.

Bashier, R. (1990). Socio-psychological factors in electronic networking. *International Journal of Lifelong Education* 9(1): 49–64.

Bautista, R. O. (1999). Staking their claim: Women, electronic networking and training in Asia. In W. Harcourt, ed., *Women@Internet: Creating New Cultures in Cyberspace*, 173–83. London and New York: Zed Books.

Baym, N. K. (1998). The emergence of on-line community. In S. G. Jones, ed., *Cybersociety 2.0: Revisiting Computer-mediated Communication and Community*, 35–68. Thousand Oaks, Calif.: Sage.

Beasley, C. (2008). Rethinking hegemonic masculinity in a globalizing world. *Men and Masculinities* 11(1): 86–103.

Benedict, H. (1992). *Virgin or Vamp? How the Press Covers Sex Crimes*. Oxford: Oxford University Press.

Bennett Jones, O. (2007, December 29). Face-to-face with Benazir Bhutto. news.bbc.co.uk/1/hi/programmes/from_our_own_correspondent/7163958 .stm (accessed December 30, 2007).

Bennett, W. L. (1997). Cracking the news code: Some rules that journalists live by. In S. Iyenagar and R. Reeves, eds., *Do the Media Govern? Politicians, Voters and Reporters in America*, 103–17. Thousand Oaks, Calif.: Sage.

Benwell, B., ed. (2003). *Masculinity and Men's Lifestyle Magazines*. Oxford: Blackwell.

Berens, J. (2002). Welcome to the pleasure Sloane. *Tatler* 297(1): 94–99.

Berns, N. (1999). My problem and how I solved it: Domestic violence in women's magazines. *Sociological Quarterly* 40(1): 85–108.

Bessenoff, G. A. (2006). Can the media affect us? Social comparison, self-discrepancy and the thin ideal. *Psychology of Women Quarterly* 39(3): 239–51.

Bimber, B. (2000). Measuring the gender gap on the Internet. *Social Science Quarterly* 81: 868–76.

Blair, K. L., Gajjalaand, R., and Tulley, C. (2008). *Webbing Cyberfeminist Practice: Communities, Pedagogies, and Social Action*. Cresskill, N.J.: Hampton Press.

Bloch, J. (2001). The new and improved Clint Eastwood: Change and persistence in Promise Keepers self-help literature. In R. H. Williams, ed., *Promise Keepers and the New Masculinity: Private Lives and Public Morality*, 11–32. Lanham, Md.: Lexington Books.

Blood, S. K. (2005). *Body Work: The Social Construction of Women's Body Image*. London and New York: Routledge.

Bly, R. (1990). *Iron John*. New York: Addison-Wesley.

Boni, F. (2002). Framing media masculinities: Men's lifestyle magazines and the biopolitics of the male body. *European Journal of Communication* 17(4): 465–78.

Borland, H., and Akram, S. (2007). Age is no barrier to wanting to look good: Women on body image, age and advertising. *Qualitative Market Research* 10(3): 310–33.

Bosely, S. (2007, December 4). Obesity is an increasing risk in childbirth report warns. *Guardian,* www.guardian.co.uk/society/2007/dec/04/health (accessed December 4, 2007).

Bowker, N. I. (1999). Convention or innovation: To what extent do chatroom users reconstruct their social identity? Master's thesis, Victoria University of Wellington, New Zealand.

Bowker, N. I., and Liu, J. (2001). Are women occupying positions of power online? Demographics of chatroom operators. *CyberPsychology and Behavior* 4(5): 631–50.

Boyle, K. (2006). *Media and Violence.* Thousand Oaks, Calif.: Sage.

Brewer, P. R. (2007). Anchors away: Media framing of broadcast television network evening news anchors. *Harvard International Journal of Press/Politics* 12(4): 3–19.

Brody, J. E. (1985, February 14). Panel terms obesity a major U.S. killer needing top priority. *New York Times,* A1.

Bronstein, C. (2008). No more black and blue: Women against violence against women and the Warner Communications boycott, 1976–1979. *Violence against Women* 14(4): 418–36.

Bryce, J., and Rutter, J. (2003). The gendering of computer gaming: Experience and space. In S. Fleming and I. Jones, eds., *Leisure Culture: Investigations.* Eastborne, UK: Leisure Studies Association.

Buchanan, R. (1991). Electing a President: The Markle Commission's Report on Campaign '88. Austin: University of Texas Press.

Burrell, I. (2004, January 10). Men offered nudes or hard news in the battle of the weeklies. *Independent,* 8.

Burstyn, V., ed. (1985). *Women against Censorship.* Vancouver: Douglas & McIntyre.

Butler, D., and Kavanagh, D. (1997). *The British General Election of 1997.* London: Macmillan.

Butler, J. (1990). Gender Trouble: Feminism and the Subversion of Identity. New York and London: Routledge.

———. (1997). Performative acts and gender constitution: An essay in phenomenology and feminist theory. In K. Conboy, N. Medina, and S. Stanbury, eds., *Writing on the Body: Female Embodiment and Feminist Theory,* 401–17. New York: Columbia University Press.

———. (2004). *Undoing Gender.* New York and Oxford: Routledge.

Byerly, C. M. (2001). The deeper structures of storytelling: Women, media corporations and the task of communication researchers. *Intersections* 1(2): 63–68.

———. (2004). Feminist intervention in newsrooms. In C. M. Byerly and K. Ross, eds., *Women and Media: International Perspectives*. Malden, Mass.: Blackwell Publishing.

Byerly, C. M., and Ross, K. (2006). *Women and Media: A Critical Introduction*. Malden, Mass.: Blackwell Publishing.

Byerly, C. M., and Warren, C. A. (1996). At the margins of centre: Organized protest in the newsroom. *Critical Studies in Mass Communication* 13(1): 1–23.

Bystrom, D. G., Banwart, M. C., Kaid, L. L., and Robertson, T. A. (2004). *Gender and Candidate Communication*. New York and London: Routledge.

Campbell, D. (2007, April 22). Never knowingly undersold. *Observer*, 3.

Campbell, D., and Asthana, A. (2007). Catwalk Ban for Under-16 Models. *Observer*, 8 July: 4.

Caplan, S. E. (2005). A social skill account of problematic Internet use. *Journal of Communication* 55(4): 721–36.

Carnes, P. J. (2002). The fire next time: Implications of changes in our understanding of human sexuality. Presentation at the National Council on Sexual Addiction and Compulsivity Conference, Nashville.

Carr, D. (2005). Contexts, gaming pleasures and gender preferences. *Simulation & Gaming* 36(5): 464–82.

Carroll, H. (2008). Men's soaps. *Television and New Media* 9(4): 263–83.

Carter, C., Branston, G., and Allan, S. eds. (1998). *News, Gender and Power*. London: Routledge.

Carter, C., and Weaver, K. (2003). *Violence and the Media*. Buckingham: Open University Press.

Cassell, J. (2002). Genderizing HCI. In J. Jacko and A. Sears, eds., *The Handbook of Human-Computer Interaction*, 402–11. Mahwah, N.J.: Lawrence Erlbaum.

Cassidy, M. F. (2001). Cyberspace meets domestic space: Personal computers, women's work and the gendered territories of the family home. *Critical Studies in Media Communication* 18(1): 44–65.

Castells, M. (1996). *The Rise of the Network Society*. Oxford and Malden, Mass.: Blackwell.

Chalaby, J. K. (2000). New media, new freedoms, new threats. *International Communication Gazette* 62(1): 19–29.

Chambers, D., Steiner, L., and Fleming, C. (2004). *Women and Journalism*. London: Routledge.

Cochrane, K. (2005) Is this your idea of glamour? *Guardian*, 15 Nov: 24.

Connell, R. W. (1995). *Masculinities*. Cambridge: Polity Press.

——. (2000). *The Men and the Boys*. Berkeley and Los Angeles: University of California Press.

Cooks, L. M., and Isgro, K. (2003). A space less travelled: Position gender in information and communication technology (ICT) development. *Feminist Media Studies* 3(3): 347–52.

Cooper, A., Delmonico, D., and Burg, R. (2000). Cybersex users, abusers, and compulsives: New findings and implications. *Sexual Addiction & Compulsivity* 7: 5–30.

Cottle, S., ed. (2003a). *News, Public Relations and Power*. London: Sage.

——, ed. (2003b). *Media Organization and Production*. London: Sage.

Coupland, J. (2007). Gendered discourses on the "problem" of ageing: Consumerized solutions. *Discourse & Communication* 1(1): 37–61.

Covert, J. J., and Dixon, T. L. (2008). A changing view: Representation and effects of the portrayal of women of color in mainstream women's magazines. *Communication Research* 35(2): 232–56.

Coward, R. (1984). *Female Desire*. London: Paladin.

Cresser, F., Gunn, L., and Balme, H. (2001). Women's experiences of online e-zine publication. *Media, Culture & Society* 23(4): 457–73.

Croteau, D., and Hoynes, W. (2001). The Business of Media: Corporate Media and the Public Interest. London: Sage.

Cuklanz, L. M. (1996). Rape on Trial: How the Mass Media Construct Legal Reform and Social Change. Philadelphia: University of Pennsylvania Press.

——. (2000). Rape on Prime Time: Television, Masculinity and Sexual Violence. Philadelphia. University of Pennsylvania Press.

Cummings, J. N., and Kraut, R. (2002). Domesticating computers and the Internet. *Information Society* 18: 221–31.

Curtis, P. (1995). Mudding: Social phenomena in text-based virtual realities. In P. Ludlow, ed., *High Noon on the Electronic Frontier: Conceptual Issues in Cyberspace*, 347–56. Cambridge, Mass.: MIT Press.

de Bruin, M. (2000). Gender, organizational and professional identities in journalism. *Journalism: Theory, Practice and Criticism* 1(2): 239–60.

de Bruin, M., and Ross, K. eds. (2004). *Gender and Newsroom Cultures: Identities at Work*. Cresskill, N.J.: Hampton Press.

Dede, C. (1996). Emerging technologies and distributed learning. *American Journal of Distance* Education 10: 4–36.

Delano Brown, J., Bybee, C. R., Wearden, S. T., and Straughan, D. M. (1987). Invisible power: Newspaper news sources and the limits of diversity. *Journalism Quarterly* 64(Spring): 50.

Delmonico, D. (2002). Sex on the superhighway: Understanding and treating cybersex addiction. In P. J. Carnes and K. M. Adams, eds., *Clinical Management of Sex Addiction*, 239–54. New York: Brunner-Routledge.

Dickerson, S. S. (2003). Gender differences in stories of everyday Internet use. *Health Care for Women International* 24: 432–51.

Downs, D. (1987). The attorney general's commission and the new politics of pornography. *American Bar Foundation Research Journal* 4: 641–79.

Duerden, N. (2006) Angel is a centrefold. *Sunday Review*, 26 Nov: 8.

Duke, L. L. (2000). Black in a blonde world: Race and girls interpretations of the feminine ideal in teen magazines. *Journalism and Mass Communication Quarterly* 77(2): 367–92.

Durham, G. G. (2007). Myths of race and beauty in teen magazines: A semiotic analysis. In Pamela J. Creedona and Judith Cramer, eds., *Women in Mass Communication*, 3rd ed., 233–45. Thousand Oaks, Calif.: Sage.

Durham, M. K. (2001). Adolescents, the Internet and the politics of gender: A feminist case analysis. *Race, Gender & Class* 8(4): 20–41.

Durkin, S. J., Paxton, S. J., and Sorbello, M. (2007). An integrative model of the impact of exposure to idealized female images on adolescent girls' body satisfaction. *Journal of Applied Social Psychology* 37(5): 1092–117.

Dworkin, A. (1979). *Pornography: Men Possessing Women*. New York: Perigee Books.

———. (1987). *Intercourse*. New York: Free Press.

Dyer, R. (1997). *White*. New York and London: Routledge.

Eastin, M. S. (2006). Video game violence and the female game player: Self and opponent gender effects on presence and aggressive thoughts. *Human Communication Research* 32(3): 351–72.

Eating Disorders Association [EDA]. (2007). *Something's Got to Change*. London: BEAT.

Edwards, Lynne Y. (2005). Victims, villains and vixens: Teen girls and Internet crime. In S. R. Mazzarella, ed., *Girl Wide Web: Girls, the Internet and the Negotiation Of Identity*, 13–30. New York: Peter Lang.

Elliott, R., and Elliott, C. (2005). Idealized images of the male body in advertising: Reader-response exploration. *Journal of Marketing Communication* 11(1): 3–19.

Ellis, K,, Hunter, N., and Jaker, B. (1992, 3rd edition) *Caught Looking*. San Francisco, CA. Long River Books.

Emerson, S. (2000, December 21). "Talking dirty." *Guardian*, 9.

Engelin-Maddox, R. (2006). Buying a beauty standard of dreaming of a new life? Expectations associated with media ideals. *Psychology of Women Quarterly* 39(3): 258–66.

Entertainment Software Association [ESA]. (2005). Essential facts about the computer and video game industry, www.theesa.com/ (accessed July 25, 2006).

Entman, R. M. (1989). How the media affect what people think: An information processing approach. *Journal of Politics* 51: 347–70.

———. (2007). Framing bias: Media in the distribution of power. *Journal of Communication* 57(3): 163–73.

Escobar, A. (1999). Gender, place and networks: A political ecology of cyberculture. In W. Harcourt, ed., *Women@Internet: Creating New Cultures in Cyberspace*, 31–54. London and New York: Zed Books.

European Commission. (1999). *Images of Women in the Media*. Brussels: Commission of the European Communities.

Evans, H. (2008). Sexed bodies, sexualized identities, and the limits of gender. *China Information* 22(2): 361–86.

Fahmy, S. (2004). Picturing Afghan women: A content analysis of AP wire photographs during the Taliban regime. *Gazette* 66(2): 91–112.

Farwell, E., Wood, P., James, M., and Banks, K. (1999). Global networking for change: Experiences from the APC Women's Programme. In W. Harcourt, ed., *Women@Internet: Creating New Cultures in Cyberspace*, 102–13. London and New York: Zed Books.

Ferber, A. L. (2000). Racial warriors and weekend warriors: The construction of masculinity in mythopoetic and white supremacist discourse. *Men and Masculinities* 3(1): 30–56.

Ferguson, M. (1983). *Forever Feminine*. London: Heinemann.

Ferree, M. (2003). Women and the Web: Cybersex activity and implications. *Sexual and Relationship Therapy* 18(3): 385–93.

Findlen, B. (1995). Listen up: Voices from the Next Feminist Generation. Seattle: Seal.

Fisher, A. (2009) Fashion: an industry ready for change. *The Observer*, 19 April: 22.

Fiske, J. (1989) *Understanding Popular Culture*. London and New York: Routledge.

Fontaine, M. (2000). A high-tech twist: ICT access and the gender divide. *TechKnowlogia*, March/April, www.techKnowLogia.org/TKL_active_pages2/CurrentArticles/main.asp?Issue Number=4&FileType=HTML&ArticleID=94 (accessed March 16, 2007).

Foster, K. (2006, June 11). Women told, drink less to avoid rape. *Scotland on Sunday*, scotlandonsunday.scotsman.com/index.cfm?id=860222006 (accessed December 7, 2007).

Foucault, M. (1978). *The History of Sexuality. Vol. 1: An Introduction* (transl.). New York: Pantheon Books.

Fowler, J. (1995). Women in politics: A fair press? Master's thesis, University of Sheffield, United Kingdom.

FoxNews.com. (2007a, October 30). Democratic candidates intensify Hillary Clinton criticism, senator fires back. www.foxnews.com/story/0,2933,306477,00 .html (accessed April 24, 2009).

FoxNews.com. (2007b, October 30). John Edwards takes aim at Hillary Clinton character issues. www.foxnews.com/politics/2007/10/30/john-edwards-takes -aim-hillary-clinton-character-issues/ (accessed April 24, 2009).

Franklin, B. (1997). *Newzak and News Media*. London: Arnold.

———, ed. (2006). Local Journalism and Local Media: Making the Local News. London and New York: Routledge.

Fredrick, C. A. N. (1999). Feminist rhetoric in cyberspace: The ethos of feminist Usenet groups. *Information Society* 15: 187–97.

Freedman, R., and Barnouin, Kim (2007) *Skinny Bitch*. Philadelphia, PA: Running Press.

Freeman, H. (2007, May 22). Watch your step. *Guardian*, 7.

Friedman, E. J. (2003). ICT and gender equality advocacy in Latin America: Impacts of a new "utility." *Feminist Media Studies* 3(3): 356–60.

Frobish, T. (2004). Sexual profiteering and rhetorical assuagement: Examining *ethos* and identity at playboy.com. *Journal of Computer-Mediated Communication* 9(3), http://jcmc.indiana.edu/vol9/issue3/frobish.html.

Funk, J., and Buchman, D. (1996). Playing violent video and computer games and adolescent self-concept. *Journal of Communication* 46(2): 19–32.

Furnham, A., and Skae, E. (1997). Changes in stereotyped portrayal of men and women in British television advertisements. *Sex Roles* 29(3): 297–310.

Gallagher, M. (1988). *Women and Television in Europe*. Brussels: Commission of the European Communities.

———. (2001). Gender Setting: New Agendas for Media Monitoring and Advocacy. London: Zed Books.

Gauntlett, D. (2002). Media, Gender and Identity: An Introduction. London: Routledge.

Geertsema, M. (2009) Women and news. *Feminist Media Studies* 9(2): 149-172.

Genderlinks (2003) *Gender and Media Baseline Study*. Johannesburg: Genderlinks.

Gibson, W. (1984). *Neuromancer*. New York: Ace Books.

Gill, R. (2007). *Gender and the Media*. Cambridge: Polity Press.

———. (2008). Sexism/empowerment figuring female sexual agency in contemporary advertising. *Feminism and Psychology* 18(1): 35–60.

———. (2009a). Beyond the "sexualization of culture" thesis: An intersectional analysis of "sixpacks," "midriffs" and "hot lesbians" in advertising. *Sexualities* 12(2): 137–60.

———. (2009b). Supersexualize me! Advertising, (post)feminism and "the midriffs." In F. B. Attwood, ed., *Mainstreaming Sex: The Sexualization of Western Culture*. London: I. B. Tauris.

Gill, R., Henwood, K., and Mclean, C. (2005). Body projects: The normative regulation of masculinity. *Body and Society* 11(1): 37–63.

Gillis, S., and Coleman, R. (2008). Feminism and Popular Culture: Explorations in Post-Feminism. London: I. B. Tauris.

Gillwald, A. (1994). Women, democracy and media in South Africa. *Media Development* 2: 27–32.

Gittler, A. M. (1999). Mapping women's global communications and networking. In W. Harcourt, ed., *Women@Internet: Creating New Cultures in Cyberspace*, 91–101. London and New York: Zed Books.

Goffman, I. (1979). *Gender Advertisements*. London: Macmillan.

Goldman, R. (1992). *Reading Ads Socially*. London and New York: Routledge.

Goldman, R., Heath, D., and Smith, S. L. (1991). Commodity feminism. *Critical Studies in Mass Communication* 8(4): 333–51.

Gorriz, C. M., and Medina, C. (2000). Engaging girls with computers through software games. *Communications of the ACM* 34 (1): 42–49.

Graphics, Visualization and Useability Center [GVU]. (1998). *The Tenth WWW User Survey*. Georgia Institute of Technology, www.gvu.gatech/edu/usersurveys/survey-1998-10/ (accessed May 18, 2007) Grisso, A. D., and Weiss, D. (2005). What are gURLs talking about? Adolescent girls' construction of sexual identity on gURL.com. In S. R. Mazzarella, ed., *Girl Wide Web: Girls, the Internet and the Negotiation of Identity*, 31–49. New York: Peter Lang.

Grogan S. (1999). Body Image: Understanding Body Dissatisfaction in Men, Women and Children. New York: Routledge.

Gurer, D., and Camp, T. (2002). An ACM-W literature review on women in computing. *SIGSCE Bulletin* 34(2): 121–27.

Gutfeld, G. (1999). The sex drive. *Men's Health* 14(8), 116–124.

Haddon, L. (1999). Gender and the domestication of the home computer: A look back. In W. H. Dutton, ed., *Society on the Line: Information Politics in the Digital Age*, 253–54. New York: Oxford University Press.

Hall, B. E. (2002). Blogs by women. ringsaround.net/womenbloggers (accessed May 18, 2007).

Hall, K. (1996). Cyberfeminism. In S. Herring, ed., *Computer-Mediated Communication: Linguistic, Social and Cross-Cultural Perspectives*, 147–70. Amsterdam: Benjamins.

Hall, S. (1973). *Encoding and Decoding in the Television Discourse*. CCCS Occasional Paper # 7. Birmingham: Centre for Contemporary Cultural Studies.

———. (1997) The work of representation. In S. Hall, ed. *Representation: Cultural Representations and Signifying Practices*. London, Thousand Oaks and New Delhi: Sage: 13-74.

Hall, S. ed. (1997) *Representation: Cultural Representations and Signifying Practices*. London, Thousand Oaks and New Delhi: Sage.

Halliwell, E., and Dittmar, H. (2003). A qualitative investigation of women's and men's body image concerns and their attitudes toward ageing. *Sex Roles* 49(11/12): 675–84.

Harcourt, W. (1999a). WoN weaving together the virtual and the actual. In W. Harcourt, ed., *Women@Internet: Creating New Cultures in Cyberspace*, 220–25. London and New York: Zed Books.

———, ed. (1999b). *Women@Internet: Creating New Cultures in Cyberspace*. London and New York: Zed Books.

———. (2000). The personal and the political: Women using the Internet. *CyberPsychology & Behavior* 3(5): 693–98.

Haraway, D. (1997). Modest_Witness@Second_Millennium. Female Man Meets Onco Mouse. London: Routledge.

Harrison, K. (2000). The body electric: Thin-ideal media and eating disorders in adolescents. *Journal of Communication* 50(3): 119–43.

Hartmann, T., and Klimmt, C. (2006). Gender and computer games: Exploring females' dislikes. *Journal of Computer-Generated Communication* 11(4) article 2.

Hassan, R. (2004). *Media, Politics and the Network Society*. Maidenhead, U.K.: Open University Press.

Hawthorne, S., and Klein, R., eds. (1999). *Cyberfeminism: Connectivity, Critique + Creativity*. Melbourne: Spinifex.

Healey, T., and Ross, K. (2002). Growing old invisibly: Older viewers talk television. *Media, Culture & Society* 24(1): 125–40.

Heeks, R. (1999). Information and communication technologies, poverty and development. Development Informatics Working Paper Series, Working Paper No. 5. Institute for Development Policy and Management, University of Manchester, www.man.ac.uk/idp (accessed May 14, 2007).

Hendry, S. (2000, December 20). Is it right to ban this ad? *Sun*, 17.

Hennessee, J., and Nicholson, J. (1972, May 28). NOW says: TV commercials insult women. *New York Times Magazine*, 12–13, 48–51.

Henry, J. M. (1998). An Africalogical analysis of the Million Man March: A look at the response to the march as a measure of its effectiveness. *Howard Journal of Communication* 9: 157–68.

Hernandez, D. (1995, July 1). Are women being annhiliated by the media? *Editor and Publisher.*

Herring, S. (1994). Politeness in computer culture. Why women thank and men flame. In M. Bucholtz, A. Liang, and L. Sutton, eds., *Communicating In, Through and Across Cultures,* 278–94. Proceedings of the Third Berkeley Women and Language conference. Berkeley: Berkeley Women and Language Group.

Herring, S. (1999). The rhetorical dynamics of gender harassment online. *The Information Society* 15: 151–67.

Hesmondhalgh, D. (2006). *Media Production.* Maidenhead, U.K.: Open University Press.

Hill, A. (2006, September 3). If you want to find true happiness, fake it. *Observer.*

Hill, S. T. (1997). Science and engineering bachelor's degrees awarded to women increase overall, but decline in several fields. www.nsf/gov/sbe/datafrf/sdb97326 (accessed May 8, 2007).

Hill-Collins, P. (1990). *Black Feminist Thought.* New York: Routledge.

Hine, C. (2001). Web pages, authors and audiences: The meaning of a mouse click. *Information, Communication and Society* 4(2): 182–98.

Hinds, H and Stacey, J. (2001) Imaging Feminism, Imaging Femininity: The Bra-Burner, Diana, and the Woman Who Kills. *Feminist Media Studies,* 1(2): 153 – 177.

Hjul, J. (2003, May 15). Why I for one, will secretly miss Clare. *Scotsman,* 14.

Holden, T. (1999). The color of difference: Critiquing cultural convergence via television advertising. *Interdisciplinary Information Sciences* 5(1): 15–36.

Howard, P., Rainie, L., and Jones, S. (2001). Days and nights on the Internet: The impact of diffusing technology. *American Behavioral Scientist* 45(3): 383–404.

Howze, J. (2008, August 29). Sarah Palin: The mum who's running for vice president. *Times Online,* timesonline.typepad.com/alphamummy/2008/08/sarah-palin-the.html (accessed April 18, 2009).

Hughes, D. (1999). The Internet and the global prostitution industry. In S. Hawthorne and R. Klein, eds., *Cyberfeminism: Connectivity, Critique + Creativity,* 157–84. Melbourne: Spinifex.

Huyer, S. (1997). *Supporting Women's Use of Information Technologies for Sustainable Development.* Acacia Initiative, www.drc.ca/acacia/outputs/womenicts.html (accessed March 9, 2007).

Inyatullah, S., and Milojovic, I. (1999). Exclusion and communication in the information era: From silences to global conversation. In W. Harcourt, ed., *Women@Internet: Creating New Cultures in Cyberspace*, 76–88. London and New York: Zed Books.

Iyengar, S. (1987). Television news and citizens: Explanations of national affairs. *American Political Science Review* 81: 815–31.

———. (1991). Is Anyone Responsible? How Television Frames Public Issues. Chicago: University of Chicago Press.

Jackson, J. L., Jr. (1997). Promise Keepers: Watch as well as pray. National Organization for Women, www.now.org/issues/right/promise/jackson.html (accessed July 29, 2007).

Jackson, L. A., Ervin, K. S., Gardner, P. S., and Schmitt, N. (2001). Gender and the Internet: Women communicating and men searching. *Sex Roles* 44: 363–74.

Jackson, P. (1994). Black male: Advertising and the cultural politics of masculinity. *Gender, Place & Culture* 1(1): 49–59.

Jackson, L., Sullivan, L., and Rostker, R. (1988) Gender, gender role, and body image. *Sex Roles, 19*: 429-443.

Jackson, P., Stevenson, N., and Brooks, K. (2001). *Making Sense of Men's Magazines*. Cambridge: Polity Press.

Jacobs, K. (2007). *Netporn: DIY WebCulture and Sexual Politics*. Lanham, Md.: Rowman & Littlefield.

Janssen, M., and Jacobs, K. (2007, May 8). New times, old sex, Dutch women and their playboy vaginas. Net Porn, www.mail-archive.com/netporn-l@listcultures.org/msg00272.html (accessed June 29, 2007).

Jansz, J. (2005). The emotional appeal of violent video games for adolescent males. *Communication Theory* 15(3): 219–41.

Jochen, P., Valkenberg, P. and Schouten, A.P. (2005) Developing a model of adolescent friendship formation on the internet. CyberPsychology and Behaviour 8(5): 423-430.

Johnson-Odim, C. (1991). Common themes, different contexts. In C. Mohanty Talpede, A. Russo, and L. Torres, eds., *Third World Women and the Politics of Feminism*, 314–27. Bloomington: Indiana University Press.

Jones, A. (2009, March 25). Sarah Palin #24, Hillary Clinton #34 on "World's Most Beautiful Politicians" survey. All Headline News, www.allheadlinenews.com/articles/7014553688 (accessed April 17, 2009).

Jones, N. (1996). Soundbites and Spin Doctors: How Politicians Manipulate the Media and Vice Versa. London: Indigo.

Joseph, A. (2004, August 15). Another face of violence. *Hindu.*

Juffer, J. (1998). At Home with Pornography: Women, Sexuality and Everyday Life. New York: New York University Press.

Kahn, K. F. (1994). The distorted mirror: Press coverage of women candidates for statewide office. *Journal of Politics* 56(1): 154–74.

Kahn, K. F., and Goldenberg, E. (1997). The media: Obstacle or ally of feminists? In S. Iyengar and R. Reeves, eds., *Do the Media Govern? Politicians, Voters and Reporters in America*, 156–64. Thousand Oaks, Calif.: Sage.

Kaplan, R. (1994). The gender gap at the PC keyboard: Women use computers more than men but computer companies sell to men. *American Demographics* 16: 18.

Kember, S. (2003). *Cyberfeminism and Artificial Life*. London and New York: Routledge.

Kendall, Lori. (1998). Meaning and identity in "cyberspace": The performance of gender, class and race online. *Symbolic Interaction* 21(2): 129–53.

———. (1999). Recontextualising "cyberspace": Methodological considerations for online research. In S. Jones, ed., *Doing Internet Research: Critical Issues and Method for Examining the Net*, 57–74. London: Sage.

Kendrick, W. (1987). The Secret Museum: Pornography in Modern Culture. New York: Viking Press.

Kennedy, H. (2006). Beyond anonymity or future directions for Internet identity research. *New Media & Society* 8(6): 859–76.

Kennedy, T. L. M. (2000). An exploratory study of feminist experiences in cyberspace. *CyberPsychology & Behavior* 3(5): 707–19.

Kershnar, S. (2004). Is violation pornography bad for your soul? *Journal of Social Philosophy* 35(3): 349–66.

Kilbourne, J. (1999). Deadly Persuasion: Why Women and Girls Must Fight the Addictive Power of Advertising. New York: Free Press.

———. (2000). Can't Buy My Love: How Advertising Changes the Way We Think and Feel. New York and London: Touchstone.

King, A. B. (2001). Affective dimensions of Internet culture. *Social Science Computer Review* 19(4): 414–30.

Kitzinger, J. (1992). Sexual violence and compulsory hetereosexuality. *Feminism and Psychology* 2(3): 399–418.

———. (2004). Media coverage of sexual violence against women and children. In K. Ross and C. M. Byerly, eds., *Women and Media: International Perspectives*, 13–38. Malden, Mass.: Blackwell.

Kivikuru, U. (1997). *Women in the Media*. Unpublished report on existing research in the European Union.

Komter, A. (1991). Gender power and feminist theory. In K. Davies, M. Leigenaar, and J. Oldersma, eds., *The Gender of Power*, 42–64. London: Sage.

Korn, A., and Efrat, S. (2004). The coverage of rape in the Israeli popular press. *Violence against Women* 10(9): 1056–74.

Kotzin, M. C. (1994, March 2). Louis Farrakhan's anti-Semitism: A look at the record. *Christian Century*, 224–25.

Kraut, R., Patterson, M., and Lundmark, V. (1998). Internet paradox: A social technology that reduces social involvement and psychological well-being. *American Psychologist* 53: 1017–31.

Krotoski, A. (2004). *Chicks and Joysticks: An Exploration of Women and Gaming*. London: Entertainment and Leisure Software Publishers Association.

Kurian, P. A., and Munshi, D. (2003). Terms of empowerment: Gender, ecology and ICTS for development. *Feminist Media Studies* 3(3): 352–55.

Labre, M. P. (2005). The male body ideal: Perspectives of readers and non-readers of fitness magazines. *Journal of Men's Health & Gender* 2(2): 223–29.

Lagesen, V. A. (2008). A cyberfeminist utopia? Perceptions of gender and computer science among Malaysian women computer science students and faculty. *Science, Technology & Human Values* 33(1): 5–27.

LaRose, R., Eastin, M. S., and Gregg, J. (2001). Reformatting the Internet paradox: Social cognitive explanations of internet use and depression. *Journal of Online Behavior* 1/2[Online]. Available at www.behavior.net/JOB/v1n2/paradox.html, accessed September 16, 2009.

Laurel, B. (1998). Keynote address: Technological humanism and values-driven design. Paper presented at CHI-98, Los Angeles, April 18–23.

Lawrence, R. G. (2004). Framing obesity: The evolution of news discourse on a public health issue. *Harvard International Journal of Press/Politics* 9(3): 56–75.

Leahy, Terry. (1994). Taking up a position: Discourses of femininity and adolescence in the context of man/girl relationships. *Gender & Society* 15(1): 48–72.

Lederer, L. (1980). *Take Back the Night: Women on Pornography*. New York: Harper Collins.

Lee, A. M., and Lee, S. (1996). Disordered eating and its psychosocial correlates among Chinese adolescent females in Hong Kong. *International Journal of Eating Disorders*, 20: 177–183.

Lees, S. (1995). Media reporting of rape: The 1993 British date-rape controversy. In D. Kidd Hewitt and R. Osbourne, eds., *Crime and Media: The Post-Modern Spectacle*, 107–130. London: Pluto Press.

Leibler, C., and Smith, S. J. (1997). Tracking gender differences: A comparative analysis of network correspondents and their sources. *Journal of Broadcasting and Electronic Media* 41(Winter): 58–68.

Lemish, D. (2000). The whore and the Other: Israeli images of female immigrants from the former USSR. *Gender and Society* 14(2): 339–49.

———. (2004). Exclusion and marginality: Portrayals of women in Israeli media. In K. Ross and C. M. Byerly, eds., *Women and Media: International Perspectives*, 39–59. Malden, Mass.: Blackwell.

Lemish, D., and Drob, G. (2002). All the time his wife: Portrayals of first ladies in the Israeli press. *Parliamentary Affairs* 55(1): 129–42.

Lengel, L. (1998). Access to the Internet in East Central and South-Eastern Europe. *Convergence: The International Journal of Research into New Media Technologies* 4(2): 38–55.

Lenhart, A., Rainie, L., and Lewis, O. (2001). Teenage life online: The rise of the instant-message-generation and the Internet's impact on friendships and family relationships. Pew Internet and American Life Project, pewinternet .org (accessed April 20, 2007).

Levine, D. (1998). *The Joy of Cybersex: A Guide for Creative Lovers*. New York: Ballantine Books.

Levy, Ariel. (2005). Female Chauvinist Pigs: Women and the Rise of Raunch Culture. London: Pocket Books.

Lewis, J., Inthorn, S., and Wahl-Jorgensen, K. (2005). *Citizens or Consumers? What the Media Tell Us about Political Participation*. Maidenhead, U.K.: Open University Press.

Lin, C. (1999). The portrayal of women in television advertising. In M. Myers, ed., *Mediated Women: Representations in Popular Culture*, 253–70. Cresskill, N.J.: Hampton Press.

Liran-Alper, D. (1994). Media representation of women in politics: Are they still domineering dowagers and scheming concubines? Paper presented at the International Association of Media and Communication Research annual conference, Seoul, July.

Livingston, D. J. (2007). Overcoming heterosexual anxiety before gay theology. *Theology and Sexuality* 14(1): 81–88.

Livingstone, S. (2004). A Commentary on the Research Evidence Regarding the Effects of Food Promotion on Children. London: London School of Economics.

Livingstone, S., and Green, G. (1986). Television advertising and the portrayal of gender. *British Journal of Social Psychology* 25: 149–54.

Lloyd, J. (2001, January 29). Come on: Look at me. *New Statesman*, 13–15.

Lockhart, W. H. (2001). "We are one life," but not of one gender ideology: Unity, ambiguity and the Promise Keepers. In R. H. Williams, ed., *Promise Keepers and the New Masculinity: Private Lives and Public Morality*, 73–92. Lanham, Md.: Lexington Books.

Lovdal, L. T. (1989). Sex role messages in television commercials: An update. *Sex Roles* 21: 715–24.

Lucas, K., and Sherry, J. L. (2004). Sex differences in video game play: A communication-based explanation. *Communication Research* 31(5): 499–523.

Lünenborg, M. (1996). *Journalists in Europe: An International Comparative Study* (transl.). Weisbaden: Westdeutsche Verlag.

Lyons, A. C., and Willott, S. (1999). From suet pudding to superhero: Representations of men's health for women. *Health* 3(3): 283–302.

MacAskill, E. (2008, October 4). Republican spirits lifted but polls tell different story. *Guardian*, 24.

MacKinnon, C. (1987). *Feminism Unmodified: Discourses on Life and Law.* Cambridge, Mass.: Harvard University Press.

Magnuson, E. (2007). Creating culture in the mythopoetic men's movement: An ethnographic study of micro-level leadership and socialization. *Journal of Men's Studies* 15(1): 31–56.

———. (2008). Rejecting the American dream: Men creating alternative life goals. *Journal of Contemporary Ethnography* 37(3): 255–90.

Malamuth, N. (1981). Rape proclivity among males. *Journal of Social Issues* 37: 138–57.

Maloney, C. J. (2009, April 6). Sarah Palin's ass or: How I learned to start worrying and hate the bomb. LewRockwell.com, www.lewrockwell.com/orig8/maloney9.html (accessed April 17, 2009).

Manning, P. (2001). News and News Sources: A Critical Introduction. London: Sage.

Markham, A. (1998). Life Online: Researching Real Experiences in Virtual Space. Walnut Creek, Calif.: AltaMira Press.

Marvin, C, (1988). When Old Technologies Were New: Thinking about Communications in the Late 19th Century. Oxford: Oxford University Press.

Mason, P., and Monckton-Smith, J. (2008). Conflation, collocation and confusion: British press coverage of the sexual murder of women. *Journalism* 9(6): 691–710.

Mason-Grant, J. (2004). *Pornography Embodied: From Speech to Sexual Practice*. Oxford: Rowman & Littlefield.

May, C. (1998). Capital, knowledge and ownership: The "information society" and intellectual property. *Information, Communication & Society* 1(3): 246–69.

Mazzarella, S. R., ed. (2005). Girl Wide Web: Girls, the Internet and the Negotiation of Identity. New York: Peter Lang.

Mbambo, B. (1999). Disseminating African women's information on the Internet: Issues and constraints. *Information Development* 15(2): 103–5.

McCormick, N. B., and Leonard, J. (1996). Gender and sexuality in the cyberspace frontier. *Women and Therapy* 19(4):109–19.

McCracken, E. (1993). *Decoding Women's Magazines: From Mademoiselle to Ms.* New York: St. Martin's Press.

McDougall, L. (1998). *Westminster Women.* London: Vintage.

McEwan, M. (2009, February 20). Still just a woman. *Guardian Online*, www
.guardian.co.uk/commentisfree/cifamerica/2009/feb/19/us-media-women
-hillary-clinton (accessed April 20, 2009).

McGerty, L-J. (2000). "Nobody lives only in cyberspace": Gendered subjectivities and domestic use of the Internet. *CyberPsychology & Behavior* 3(5): 895–915.

McNair, B. (2002). Striptease Culture: Sex, Media and the Democratization of Desire. London: Routledge.

———. (2006). Cultural Chaos: Journalism, News and Power in a Globalised World. London and New York: Routledge.

McNair, B., Hibberd, M., and Schlesinger, P. (2003). *Mediated Access: Broadcasting and Democratic Participation in the Age of Media Politics.* Luton, U.K.: University of Luton Press.

McPherson, T. (2000). I'll take my stand in Dixie-net: White guys, the South and cyberspace. In B. E. Kolko, L. Nakamura, and G. B. Rodman, eds., *Race in Cyberspace*, 117–32. New York: Routledge.

McRobbie, A. (2004). Post-feminism and popular culture. *Feminist Media Studies* 4(3): 255–64.

MediaWatch. (1995). *Global Media Monitoring Project: Women's Participation in the News.* Ontario: National Watch on Images of Women/MediaWatch.

Meehan, E. R., and Riordan, E. (2002). *Sex and Money: Feminism and Political Economy in the Media.* Minneapolis and London: University of Minnesota Press.

Melin-Higgins, M. (2004). Coping with journalism: Gendered newsroom culture in Britain. In M. de Bruin and K. Ross, eds., *Gender and Newsroom Cultures: Identities at Work*, 197–222. Cresskill, N.J.: Hampton Press.

Melin-Higgins, M., and Djerf-Pierre, M. (1998). Newsworking in newsrooms: Journalists and gender cultures. Paper presented at the International Association of Media and Communication Research annual conference, Glasgow, July.

Merskin, D. (2005). Making an about-face: Jammer girls and the World Wide Web. In S. R. Mazzarella, ed., *Girl Wide Web: Girls, the Internet and the Negotiation of Identity*, 51–67. New York: Peter Lang.

Messner, M. A. (1997). *Politics of Masculinities: Men in Movements.* Thousand Oaks, Calif.: Sage.

Meyer, C. (1999). Women and the Internet. *Texas Journal of Women and the Law* 8: 305–25.

Meyers, M. (1997) *News coverage of violence against women.* Newbury Park, CA, London and New Delhi. Sage.

———. (2004). Crack mothers in the news: A narrative of paternalistic racism. *Journal of Communication Inquiry* 28(3): 194–216.

Michielsens, M. (1991). *Women in View: How Does BRTN Portray Women? An Audience Survey.* Brussels: BRTN/Commission of the European Communities.

Miles, A. (2007, May 2). Where are all the women in public debate? *Times*, www.timesonline.co.uk/tol/comment/columnists/alice_miles/article1733682 .ece (accessed December 7, 2007).

Millar, M. S. (1998). *Cracking the Gender Code: Who Rules the Wired World.* Toronto: Second Story Press.

Miller, K. (1990). *A Place in the News: From Women's Pages to the Front Page.* New York: Columbia University Press.

Miller, M. (2000). Surf's up, IQs down: Top 50 web searches. *Kansas City Business Journal* 18:16.

Minahan, S., and Wolfram Cox, S. (2007). Stitch 'n' bitch: Cyberfeminism, a third place and the new materiality. *Journal of Material Culture* 12(1): 5–21.

Moghadam, V. M. (2005). *Globalizing Women: Transnational Feminist Networks.* Baltimore: Johns Hopkins University Press.

Monro, F., and Huon, G. (2005). Media-portrayed idealized images, body shame and appearance anxiety. *International Journal of Eating Disorders* 38(1): 85–90.

Morahan-Martin, J. (1998). Males, females and the Internet. In J. Gackenbach, J., ed., *Psychology and the Internet*, 169–87. San Diego: Academic Press.

———. (2000). Women and the Internet: Promises and perils. *CyberPsychology and Behavior* 3(5): 683–92.

Morahan-Martin, J., and Schumacher, P. (2000). Incidence and correlates of pathological Internet use among college students. *Computers in Human Behavior* 16: 13–29.

Morgan, R. (1980). Theory and practice: Pornography and rape. In L. Lederer, ed., *Take Back the Night: Women on Pornography.* New York: Morrow.

Mudhai, O. F. (2001). The Internet: Triumphs and trials for Kenyan journalism. In M. B. Robins and R. L. Hilliard, eds., *Beyond Boundaries: Africa in Cyberspace.* Westport, Conn.: Greenwood Press.

Munévar M. D. I., and Aburto Arrieta, J. (2002). Gender-Net: A political goal of communication technologies. *Gender, Technology and Development* 6(1): 43–62.

National Academy of Sciences. (2002). *Youth, Pornography, and the Internet.* Washington, D.C.: Academies Press.

Negroponte, N. (1995). *Being Digital.* London: Hodder & Staughton.

Newsom, V. A. (2003). Contained empowerment: A study of online feminism. Paper presented at the Computer-supported Social Interaction conference, Miami University, Ohio, April 26–28.

Newsom, V. A. and Lengel, L. (2003) The power of the weblogged word: contained empowerment in the Middle East North Africa region. *Feminist Media Studies* 3(3): 360-363.

New York Times. (1995, October 17). Powell praises marchers but denounces Farrakhan. A20.

Norris, P. (1997a). Women leaders worldwide: A splash of colour in the photo op. In P. Norris, ed., *Women, Media and Politics*, 149–65. New York: Oxford University Press.

———. ed. (1997b). *Women, Media and Politics.* New York: Oxford University Press.

———. (2001). Digital Divide: Civic Engagement, Information Poverty and the Internet Worldwide. New York: Cambridge University Press.

———. (2004). Electoral Engineering: Voting Rules and Political Behavior. Cambridge: Cambridge University Press.

North, L. (2007). Just a little bit of cheeky ribaldry. *Feminist Media Studies* 7(1): 81–96.

NOS Gender Portrayal Department. (1995). Interview techniques on male and female guests in Dutch current affairs features. Hilversun, Netherlands: NOS.

Nulens, G., and Audenhove, L. V. (1999). An information society in Africa? An analysis of the information society policy of the World Bank, ITU and ECA. *Gazette* 61(6): 451–71.

Nyabuga, G. (2007). Unfulfilled potential: A cyber-realistic assessment of the impact of the Internet on Kenya politics. Ph.D. diss., Coventry University, UK.

Odell, P. M., Korgen, K. O., Schumacher, P., and Delucchi, M. (2000). Internet use among female and male college students. *CyberPsychology & Behavior* 3(5): 855–62.

Ono, H., and Zavodny, M. (2003). Gender and the Internet. *Social Science Quarterly* 8(4): 111–21.

Opoku-Mensah, A. (2004). Hanging there: Women, gender and newsroom culture. In M. de Bruin and K. Ross, eds., *Gender and Newsroom Cultures: Identities at Work*, 107–20. Cresskill, N.J.: Hampton Press.

Orbach, S. (1978). *Fat Is a Feminist Issue.* London: Arrow Books.

Orr, D. (2005). Floundering in the macho media. *British Journalism Review* 16(4): 61–67.

Paletz, D. (1988). Pornography, politics and the press: The US Attorney General's Commission on Pornography—an essay review. *Journal of Communication* 38(2): 122–36.

Pauley, J. L. (1998). Reshaping public persona and the prophetic ethos: Louis Farrakhan at the Million Man March. *Western Journal of Communication* 62(4): 512–36.

Pedersen, I. (2002). Looking good on whose terms? Ambiguity in two Kellogg's Special K® print advertisements. *Social Semiotics* 12(2): 169–81.

Peter, J., and Valkenburg, P. M. (2006). Individual differences in perceptions of Internet communication. *European Journal of Communication* 21(2): 213–26.

Pilkington, E. (2009a, January 10). Palin attacks media for her treatment during election race. *Guardian*, 21.

———. (2009b, March 12). Palin's family drama not likely to halt political ambitions. *Guardian Online*, www.guardian.co.uk/world/2009/mar/12/sarah-palin-bristol-levi-republicans (accessed April 18, 2009).

Plant, S. (1997). Zeros + Ones: Digital Women and the New Technoculture. London: Fourth Estate.

Plous, S., and Neptune, D. (1997). Racial and gender biases in magazine advertising: a content-analytic study. *Psychology of Women Quarterly* 21(4): 627–44.

Podlas, K. (2000). Mistresses of their domain: How female entrepreneurs in cyberporn are initiating a gender power shift. *CyberPsychology & Behavior* 3(5): 847–54.

Poindexter, P.M., Meraz, S. and Schmitz, A. (2008) *Women, Men and News: Divided and Disconnected in the News Media Landscape.* New York: Routledge.

Pountain, D., and Robins, D. (2000). *Cool Rules: Anatomy of an Attitude.* London: Reaktion Books.

Rake, K. (2006, August 8). Let's reclaim the f-word. *Guardian*, www.guardian.co.uk/commentisfree/story/0,,1839482,00.html (accessed December 29, 2007).

Ramp, S. (1999). *The positive power of porn.* Fairfield County Weekly, www.fairfieldweekly.com/articles/porn.html (accessed June 20, 2007).

Raphael, C., Bachen, C., Lynn, K-M, Baldwin-Phillippi, J., and McKee, K. A. (2006). Portrayals of information and communication technology on World Wide Web sites for girls. *Journal of Computer-Mediated Communication* 11(3): 771–801.

Rea, M. (2001) What is pornography? *Nous* 35(1): 118-145.

Redmond, S. (2003). Thin white women in advertising: Deathly corporeality. *Journal of Consumer Culture* 3(2): 170–90.

Rheingold, H. (1993). The Virtual Community: Homesteading on the Electronic Frontier. Reading, Mass.: Addison-Wesley.

Rhodes, J. (1995). The visibility of race and media history. In G. Dines and J. Humez, eds., *Gender, Race and Class in Media: A Text Reader*, 33–42. Thousand Oaks, Calif.: Sage.

Roberts, L. D., and Parks, M. R. (2001). The social geography of gender-switching in virtual environments on the Internet. In E. Green and A. Adam, eds., *Virtual Gender: Technology, Consumption and Identity*, 265–85. London: Routledge.

Robins, M. (2002). Are African women online just ICT consumers? *Gazette: the International Journal for Communication Studies* 64(3): 235–49.

Robinson, G. J. (2005). Gender, Journalism and Equity: Canadian, U.S. and European Perspectives. Cresskill, N.J.: Hampton Press.

Rodgers, S., and Thorson, E. (2003). A socialization perspective on male and female reporting. *Journal of Communication* 53(4): 658–75.

Rogers, A. (2005). Chaos to control: Men's magazines and the mastering of intimacy. *Men and Masculinities* 8(2): 175–94.

Romano, L. (2009) Clinton puts up a new fight. *The Washington Post*, 20 May: C01.

Rondino, M. (1997). Breaking out of binaries. Reconceptualizing gender and its relationship to computer mediated communication. *Journal of Computer Mediated Communication* 3(3), www.ascusc.org/jcmc/vol3/issue3/Rondino/html (accessed December 31, 2007).

Root, J. (1986). *Open the Box: About Television*. Comedia Series 34. London: Channel Four and Comedia.

Ross, K. (1995a). Black and White Media: Black Images in Popular Film and Television. Cambridge: Polity Press.

———. (1995b). Skirting the issue: Political women and the media. *Everywoman* 199: 16–17.

———. (1997). "But where's me in it?" Disability, broadcasting and the audience. *Media, Culture & Society* 19(4): 669–77.

———. (2001). Women at work: Journalism as en-gendered practice. *Journalism Studies* 2(4): 531–44.

———. (2002). Women, Politics, Media: Uneasy Relations in Comparative Perspective. Cresskill, N.J.: Hampton Press.

———. (2004). Political talk, radio and democratic participation: Caller perspectives on *Election Call. Media, Culture and Society* 26(6): 785–801.

———. (2005). Women in the boyzone: Gender, news and herstory. In S. Allan, ed., *Journalism: Critical Issues*, 287-298. Buckingham: Open University Press.

———. (2007). The journalist, the housewife, the citizen and the press. *Journalism* 8(4): 440–73.

Ross, K., and Sreberny-Mohammadi, A. (1997). Playing house: Gender, politics and the news media in Britian. *Media,Culture and Society* 19(1): 101–9.

Rowan, J. (1987). *The Horned God*. New York: Routledge.

Royal, C. (2008). Framing the Internet: A comparison of gendered spaces. *Social Science Computer Review* 26(2):152–69.

Rubin, G. (1984). Thinking sex: Notes for radical theory of the politics of sexuality. In C. S. Vance, ed., *Pleasure and Danger: Exploring Female Sexuality*, 268–319. London: Routledge & Kegan Paul.

Rubin, L., Nemeroff, C. J., and Russo, N. F. (2004). Exploring feminist women's body consciousness. *Psychology of Women Quarterly* 28: 27–37.

Rush, R. (2001). Three decades of women and mass communications research: The ratio of recurrent and reinforced residuum hypothesis (R3) revisited. Paper presented at Donna Allen Memorial Symposium, Freedom Forum, Rosslyn, Virginia, August 3–4.

Sanders, C. E., Field, T. M., and Diego, M. (2000). The relationship of Internet use to depression and social isolation amongst adolescents. *Adolescence* 35: 237–41.

Sanders, K. (2003). *Ethics and Journalism*. London: Sage.

Sardar, Z. (1996). alt.civilizations.faq cyberspace as the darker side of the West. In Z. Sardar and J. R. Ravertz, *Cyberfutures: Culture and Politics on the Information Highway*, 14–41. London: Pluto Press.

Sauma, L. (2007, March 4). Sisters, doing it for themselves. *ABC Magazine*, 4.

Schauer, T. (2005). Women's porno: The heterosexual female gaze in porn sites "for women." *Sexuality & Culture* 9(2): 42–64.

Schmitz, J. (1997). Structural relations, electronic media, and social change: The public electronic network and the homeless. In S. G. Jones, ed., *Virtual Culture: Identity and Communication in Cyberspace*, 80–101. London: Sage.

Scodari, C. (2005). You're sixteen, you're dutiful, you're online: "Fangirls" and the negotiation of age and/or gender subjectivities in TV newsgroups. In S. R. Mazzarella, ed., *Girl Wide Web: Girls, the Internet and the Negotiation of Identity*, 105–20. New York: Peter Lang.

Scott, A., Semmens, L., and Willoughby, L. (1999). Women and the Internet: The natural history of a research project. *Information, Communication & Society* 2(4): 541–65.

Seamark, M., and Newling, D. (2005, September 28). So much for improved security. *Daily Mail*, 9.

Seelye, K., and Bosman, J. (2008, June 13). Critics and news executives split over sexism in Clinton coverage. *New York Times Online*, www.nytimes

.com/2008/06/13/world/americas/13iht-13women.13681561.html (accessed April 18, 2009).

Segal, L. (1992). Introduction. In L. Segal and M. McIntosh, eds., *Sex Exposed: Sexuality and the Pornography Debate*, 1–11. London: Virago.

———. (2006, December 22). Being a man just ain't what it used to be. *Times Higher Education Supplement*, 18.

Semmens, L., and Willoughby, L. (1996). Will women be excluded from the "white male playground"? Paper presented at the MediaActive conference, Liverpool, June 30–July 2.

Shade, L. R. (2002). Gender and Community in the Social Construction of the Internet. New York: Peter Lang.

Shamoon, D. (2004) Office Sluts and Rebel Flowers: The Pleasure of Japanese Pornographic comics for women. In Linda Williams (ed.) *Porn Studies*. Durham and London: Duke University Press: 90-120.

Shaw, L. H., and Gant, L. M. (2002). Users divided? Exploring the gender gap in Internet use. *CyberPsychology & Behavior* 5(6): 517–36.

Shoemaker, P. J., and Reese, S. D. (1996). *Mediating the Message: Theories of Influence on Mass Media Content*, 2nd. ed. White Plains, N.Y.: Longman.

Short, C. (1991). Dear Clare . . . this is what women feel about page 3. London: Radius.

Shugart, H. A., Waggoner, C. E., and Hallstein, D. (2001). Mediating third-wave feminism: Appropriation as postmodern media practice. *Critical Studies in Media Communication* 18(2): 194–210.

Sieghart, M. A., and Henry, G. (1998). *The Cheaper Sex: How Women Lose Out in Journalism*. London: Women in Journalism.

Singh, S. (2001). Gender and the use of the Internet at home. *New Media & Society* 3(4): 395–416.

Smith, C. (2003). Fellas in fully frontal frolics: Naked men in *For Women* magazine. *Paragraph* 26(1/2): 134–46.

———. (2007a). One for the Girls: The Pleasures and Practices of Reading Women's Porn. Bristol: Intellect Books.

———. (2007b). Designed for pleasure: Style, indulgence and accessorised sex. *European Journal of Cultural Studies* 19(2): 167–84.

Smith, D. E. (1990). Texts, Facts and Femininity: Exploring the Relations of Ruling. New York: Routledge.

Soothill, K., and Walby, S. (1991). *Sex Crimes in the News*. London: Routledge.

Spady, R. (1999, November 10). Buy, sell, or hold: Playboy. The Angle.com, www.theangle.com/business/1999_1110/playboy.shtml (accessed June 20, 2007).

Spender, D. (1995). Nattering on the Net: Women, Power and Cyberspace. Melbourne: Spinifex.

Steen, F. F., Greenfield, P. M., Davies, M., and Tynes, B. (2006). What went wrong with the Sims Online: Cultural learning and barriers to identification in a massively multiplayer online role-playing game. In P. Vorderer and J. Bryant, eds., *Playing Video Games: Motives, Responses, and Consequences*, 307–24. Mahwah, N.J.: Lawrence Erlbaum Associates.

Steiner, L. (1998). Newsroom accounts of power at work. In C. Carter, G. Branston, and S. Allan, eds., *News, Gender and Power*, 145–159. London: Routledge.

Stephenson, M-A. (1998). The Glass Trapdoor: Women, Politics and the Media during the 1997 General Election. London: Fawcett Society.

Stern, S. R. (2002) Adolescent girls' expression on web home pages: Spirited, somber and self-conscious sites. *Convergence* 5: 22–41.

Stevenson, N., Jackson, P., and Brooks, K. (2000). The politics of "new" men's lifestyle magazines. *European Journal of Cultural Studies* 3(3): 366–85.

Stone, D. 1997. *Policy Paradox*. New York: Norton.

Sunden, J. (2001). What happened to difference in cyberspace? The (re)turn of the she-cyborg. *Feminist Media Studies* 1(2): 215–30.

Tannen, D. (1992). You Just Don't Understand: Women and Men in Conversation. London: Virago.

Thomas, M. E., and Treiber, L. A. (2000). Race, gender and status: A content analysis of print advertisements in four popular magazines. *Sociological Spectrum* 29(3): 357–71.

Thompsen, P. A. (1996). What's fueling the flames in cyberspace? A social influence model. In L. Strate, R. Jacobsen, and S. B. Gibson, eds., *Communication and Cyberspace: Social Interaction in an Electronic Environment*. Cresskill, NJ: Hampton Press, 297–315.

Thompson, E. (2008). The parodic sensibility and the sophisticated gaze. *Television and New Media* 9(4): 283–304.

Tincknell, E., Chambers, D., Van Loon, J., and Hudson, N. (2003). Begging for it: "New femininities," social agency and moral discourse in contemporary teenage and men's magazines. *Feminist Media Studies* 3(1): 47–63.

Tuchman, G., Daniels, A. K., and Benet, J. W. (1978) *Hearth and Home: Images of Women in the Mass Media*. Oxford: Oxford University Press.

Tufte, B. (2003). Girls in the new media landscape. *Nordicom Review* 24(1): 71–78.

Tunstall, J. (1977). *The Media Are American*. London: Constable.

Turkle, S. (1995). *Life on the Screen: Identity in the Age of the Internet*. London: Weidenfeld and Nicholson.

United Nations (1996) *Report of the Fourth World Conference on Women*, (Beijing Declaration and Platform for Action). New York: United Nations.

Valenti, J. (2007). Full Frontal Feminism: A Young Woman's Guide to Why Feminism Matters. Emeryville, Calif.: Seal Press.

Van Zoonen, L. (1998). One of the girls? The changing gender of journalism. In C. Carter, G. Branston, and S. Allan, eds., *News, Gender and Power*, 33–46. London: Routledge.

———. (2002) Gendering the Internet: Claims, controversies and cultures. *European Journal of Communication* 17(5): 5–23.

Vetten, L. (1998). Reporting on rape in South Africa. *Women's Media Watch Newsletter* 3: 5–8.

Virilio, P. (1997). *Open Sky*. London: Verso.

Vrooman, S. S. (2001). Flamethrowers, slashers and witches: Gendered communication in a virtual community. *Qualitative Research Reports in Communication* (Spring): 33–41.

Wajcman, J. (1991). *Feminism Confronts Technology*. Sydney: Allen and Unwin.

Wakeford, N. (2002). Networks of Desire: Gender, Sexuality and Computing Culture. London and New York: Routledge.

Wakunuma, K. (2007). Gender and information communication technologies (ICTs): Implications for women in developing countries. Ph.D. diss., Coventry University, United Kingdom.

Walker, R. (1995). To Be Real: Telling the Truth and Changing the Face of Feminism. New York: Anchor.

Walsh-Childer, K., Chance, G., and Herzog, K. (1996). Sexual harrassment of women journalists. *Journalism and Mass Communication Quarterly* 73(3): 559–81.

Walther, J. B., and Bunz, U. (2005). The rules of virtual groups: Trust, liking and performance in computer-mediated communication. *Journal of Communication* 55(4): 828–46.

Wasserman, I. M., and Richmond-Abbott, M. (2005). Gender and the Internet: Causes of variation in access, level and scope of use. *Social Science Quarterly* 86(1): 252–70.

Watkins, S. Craig. (2001). Framing protest: News media frames of the Million Man March. *Critical Studies in Mass Communication* 18(1): 83–101.

Weathers, H. (2005, June 28). Fathers 4 Justice? I created a monster. *Daily Mail*, 20.

Weaver, D. H. (1992, September). A secret no more. *Washington Journalism Review*, 23–27.

Whelehan, I. (2000). *Overloaded: Popular Culture and the Future of Feminism*. London: Women's Press.

———. (2004). Having it all (again). Paper presented at ESRC seminar, London School of Economics, London, November.

White, C., and Kinnick, K. N. (2000). One click forward and two clicks back: Portrayal of women using computers in television commercials. *Women's Studies in Communication* 23(3): 292–312.

Wilcox, P. (2005). Beauty and the beast: Gendered and raced discourse in the news. *Social and Legal Studies* 14(4): 515–32.

Wildman, S. (2008, November 5). Women voters weren't fooled by Sarah Palin. *Guardian Online*, www.guardian.co.uk/commentisfree/cifamerica/2008/nov/05/sarah-palin-barack-obama-women (accessed April 19, 2009).

Williams, G. (2001). Masculinity in context: An epilogue. In R. H. Williams, ed., *Promise Keepers and the New Masculinity: Private Lives and Public Morality*, 105–14. Lanham, Md.: Lexington Books.

———. (1999). *Hard Core: Power, Pleasure and the "Frenzy of the Visible,"* 2nd ed. Berkeley: University of California Press.

———, ed. (2004). *Porn Studies*. Durham, N.C. and London: Duke University Press.

Williams, R. H. (2001). Promise Keepers: A comment on religion and social movements. In R. H. Williams, ed., *Promise Keepers and the New Masculinity: Private Lives and Public Morality*, 1–10. Lanham, Md.: Lexington Books.

Williamson, J. (2003, May 31). Sexism with an alibi. *Guardian*.

Wilson, K. R., Wallin, J. S., and Reiser, C. (2003). Social stratification and the digital divide. *Social Science Computer Review* 21(2): 133–43.

Winship, J. (1987). *Inside Women's Magazines*. London: Pandora.

Wolf, N. (1990). *The Beauty Myth*. London: Chatto and Windus.

Womack, S. (2006, January 19). How crusaders for justice were zapped by the extremists. *Daily Telegraph*, 4.

Women in Journalism. (1999). *Real Women: The Hidden Sex*. London: Women in Journalism.

Wood, E. A. (2008). Consciousness-raising 2.0: Sex blogging and the creation of a feminist sex commons. *Feminism & Psychology* 18(4): 480–87.

Woolf, M. (2002). Watchdog joins attack on motor show by branding lacy bra poster 'tasteless.' *Independent*, 29 Oct, n.p. www.independent.co.uk/news/media/watchdog-joins-attack-on-motor-show-by-branding-lacy-bra-poster-tasteless-615201.html (accessed August, 8 2009).

World Association of Christian Communication [WACC]. (2000). *Global Media Monitoring Project 2000*. London: WACC.

Wörsching, M. (2007). Race to the top: Masculinity, sport, and nature in German magazine advertising. *Men and Masculinities* 10(3): 197–221.

Wykes, M. (1998). A family affair: The British press, sex and the Wests. In C. Carter, G. Branston, and S. Allan, eds., *News, Gender and Power*, 233–47. London: Routledge.

Wykes, M., and Gunter, B. (2005). *The Media and Body Image*. London: Sage.

Young, K. S. (1998). Internet addiction: The emergence of a new clinical disorder. *CyberPsychology & Behavior* 1(4): 237–44.

———. (1999). *Cybersexual addiction*. Center for Internet Addiction Recovery, www.netaddiction.com/cybersexual_addiction.htm (accessed July 1, 2007).

———. (2008). Understanding sexually deviant online behavior from an addiction perspective. *International Journal of Cyber Criminology* 2(1): 298-307.

Young, K. S., Griffin-Shelley, E., Cooper, A., O'Mara, J., and Buchanan, J. (2000). Online infidelity: A new dimension in couple relationships with implications for evaluation and treatment. *Sexual Addiction and Compulsivity* 7(1): 59–74.

Youngs, G. (1999). Virtual voices: Real lives. In W. Harcourt, ed., *Women@ Internet: Creating New Cultures in Cyberspace*, 55–75. London and New York: Zed Books.

Zernicke, K. (2003, November 9). Is obesity the responsibility of the body politic? *New York Times*, 4.

Zilliacus-Tikkanen, H. (1997). *The Essence of Journalism from a Gender Perspective* (transl.). Helsinki: Yleisradio Publications, A1.

Zoch, L. M., and VanSlyke Turk, J. (1998). Women making news: Gender as a variable in source selection and use. *Journalism and Mass Communication Quarterly* 75(4): 762–75.

Zorn, I. (2004). VIFU: Virtual community building for networking among women. *Gender, Technology and Development* 8(1): 75–95.

INDEX

Adams, D., 73
Adams-Price, C. E., 141
advertising: African Americans in,
    55–57; Asians in, 55; body shape
    and, 46–51; capitalism and, 43;
    celebrities and, 54, 55–56, 153;
    faces and, 51–52, 153; gender
    identity and, 8; guerrilla tactics
    against, 63; health and, 15–16;
    irony in, 16, 41–42; men's body
    shapes and, 52–54; of Motor
    Show, 62, 162n10; race and,
    54–57; shifts in, 43, 153; sports
    and race in, 55–56; stereotypes
    in, 43–45; violence in, 46–47; in
    women's magazines, 45, 153
Afghanistan, 94–95
Africa: Internet in, 145–48; Senegal,
    146; South Africa, 97; Southern
    Africa, 94, 97, 114, 163n4
African Americans: in advertising,
    55–57; MMM and, 25–26

ageing: faces and, 51–52; men v.
    women, 51; women journalists
    and, 117, 163n9
Allan, S., 119
Allen, Lily, 11, 31
Allende, Isabel, 160
American Chopper, 19
Andrews, Brittany, 82
Angelou, Maya, 13
anticensorship, pornography and,
    74–75
anxiety: about ideals, 42. *See also*
    eating disorders
APC. *See* Association for Progressive
    Communications
Arizpe, L., 35–36
Armstrong, Donna, 57–58, 112
art, pornography v., 67–68
Asians, in advertising, 55
Association for Progressive
    Communications (APC), 138
Attwood, F., 71

ABOUT THE AUTHOR

Karen Ross is professor of media and public communication at the University of Liverpool, UK. She teaches political communication and gender and media. She has written extensively on the relationship among women, politics, and media and has also written more broadly on aspects of media culture such as media and the public, media and identity politics, and audience studies. She has written or edited fifteen books and numerous journal articles, chapters, and conference papers. She is the foundational editor of the new ICA/Wiley-Blackwell journal, *Communication, Culture and Critique* which launched in March 2008.

Her most recent books include *The Media and the Public: 'Them' and 'Us' in Media Discourse* (with Stephen Coleman, in press); *Popular Communication: Essays on Publics, Practices and Processes* (edited, with Stuart Price, 2008); *Rethinking Media Education: Critical Pedagogy and Identity Politics* (edited, with Anita Nowak and Sue Abel, 2007); *Women and Media: A Critical Introduction* (with Carolyn Byerly, 2006); *Gender and Newsroom Practice* (edited, with Marjan de Bruin, 2004).